Growing Up Under the Third Reich

Helga Arndt and Her Sisters

Gertrude (Traute) Tatzmann, Elsbeth Helling
and Frieda Mueller

ISBN: 978-1-945975-33-3

Published by EA Books Publishing a division of
Living Parables of Central Florida, Inc. a 501c3
EABooksPublishing.com

CONTENTS

DEDICATION

In memory of

Ferdinand and Anna Lenk

"But the eyes of the LORD are on those who fear him,

On those whose hope is in his unfailing love,

to deliver them from death and keep them alive in famine."

Psalm 33:18-19 (NIV)

ACKNOWLEDGMENTS

First, I like to thank God for his protection during the terrible time of war and for giving us six siblings godly parents.

Second, I like to express my appreciation to my daughters, Corinna Arndt and Monika Arndt Sannoh, for encouraging me for many years to write an account of my childhood experiences. And Corinna—thank you very much for organizing all the photos and the other technical help.

I thank my three sisters for letting me use excerpts from their journals. Without them our family story would not have been complete.

To my nephew, Manfred Tatzmann, I like to say, "Your proofreading of several written and rewritten manuscripts was a lot of help—thank you."

Furthermore, I like to acknowledge my editor Kristen Stieffel for a job well done.

I am grateful for Cheri Cowell's influence at the Christian Writer's Conference that prompted me to go with EA Books Publishing. Thanks also for your encouragement and belief in my project.

PREFACE

In the middle of summer in 1939, I entered this world. Germany was restless. Wherever people gathered, one heard whispers of a possible war. They were correct in assuming the inevitable. World War II started the first day of September 1939, when Hitler's army invaded Poland.

The first six years of my life are very memorable, since I witnessed firsthand the destruction a war can have on a country and its people. I have two daughters, and my greatest desire was to raise them in peacetime. Thank God I was able to do it in my new adopted country, the United States of America.

However, I wanted them to know what it was like to grow up under such horrible circumstances. I am the sixth child in the Lenk family, and that is one reason I report also what my siblings experienced. So this will be a fuller picture about the whole family history from 1923, when my parents were married, to 1959, when I came to the United States.

We learned about each other's childhood and teenage experiences over many family gatherings. For cohesion and readability, I used the birthday party and the ladies luncheon as a launching pad to dive into the past.

Helga Lenk Arndt

INTRODUCTION

On my father's side, I can trace my heritage to the year 1869. That was when my grandmother, Amalie Lenk, was born in East Prussia. My father was born in 1899, also in East Prussia. I have always been proud of that fact, because I feel the East Prussians are the real Germans. I believe this feeling originated after West Germany was flooded with refugees from Ukraine and Poland after World War II.

My grandparents emigrated from East Prussia to West Germany after World War I. East Prussia was mainly farmland and suffered a lot of devastation during the war. Many families left their farms behind to seek other employment in West Germany. Many of those immigrants settled in Westphalia, because that's where the coal mines were. Job opportunities were scarce, and men accepted mining jobs to make a living.

My grandparents had nine children: six girls and three boys. One girl died of influenza at the young age of seventeen. Unfortunately, Grandpa also died prematurely, killed in an accident in the coal mine. This left Grandma to raise all those children by herself. The oldest boy was married already and out on his own. Now it was up to the second-oldest son, my father, to start working and help support the family. As the years wore on, all the girls and Papa's other brother got married. My father and mother were married in 1923.

My mother was born in 1901 in Hanover, Germany. When I was growing up, Mama told me many stories about her childhood and teenage years. Her face reflected hurtful memories when she spoke about her past.

Mama told me, "I did not have a very happy childhood. My mother died when I was only nine years old. My father remarried a widow with two boys. I tell you, Helga," she continued, "my stepmother had all the characteristics associated sometimes with the word stepmother. She treated me with contempt and could hardly wait for me to turn fourteen and finish school. That way she could find employment for me away from home."

Mama's stepmother arranged for her to work as a housemaid with a family who owned and operated an Imbiss Stube (a snack bar). When she went home sometimes on her days off, her stepmother would ask her, "What are you doing here?" I felt sad when Mama related those incidents.

While she was working there, World War I broke out. As it happened, her employer was called up to active duty in the armed forces. The owners of the business baked their own bread; now Mama had to do all the bread baking. She said, "The work was really hard, but there was nothing I could do about it. It was my job, and I don't think my stepmother would have let me break my apprenticeship contract."

My mother was an attractive woman. She had beautiful black hair, brown eyes, and a good complexion. After the owner came back from the war, he had mother work in the dining room instead of in the kitchen. Male customers began to notice her, and there was someone that Mama really liked.

However, her stepmother had her eyes on a young fellow in her circle of friends. His name was Ferdinand Lenk, and she thought he would be a good match for Anna, my mother. Arrangements were made for Ferdinand and Anna to get married.

PART ONE

Storm Rising and Arrival –Normal Childhood Denied

Chapter 1
Coming to America, 1959

The plane descended smoothly over New York's Idlewild Airport. It was not called JFK until four years later, in honor of President Kennedy. I couldn't wait to see what New York City looked like. I had seen Hollywood movies, especially crime dramas, that contained scenes set in New York or Chicago.

My sister-in-law, Renate (who with my brother Fritz, had immigrated to the United States just two years earlier), picked me up from the airport. As we drove through Manhattan, I strained my neck, looking up at all the skyscrapers. Sometimes I tried to estimate how many floors were in those tall buildings. Scenes from movies became reality. So many people, cars, taxis and storefronts! The big impression I received was that everything was in abundance. Stores next to stores, the streets full of cars and trucks, the sidewalks full of people—it was a city fully alive. What a change from a little town I grew up in!

The trip to Union City, New Jersey, where my brother lived, took almost two hours. The tall skyscrapers fell behind us once we emerged from the Lincoln Tunnel. Here the houses stood six or seven stories high, but some were gigantic apartment houses. My brother and sister-in-law lived in a three-story apartment house.

The plan for me was to stay with my brother in New Jersey until my sister and her husband came from Michigan to pick me up. That's where my three other sisters and my other brother lived. I was not only the youngest of the siblings, but also the last to immigrate to America.

The first to leave Germany was my sister Frieda with her husband, Helmut, and a baby boy in 1951. The second couple was my sister Elsbeth with her husband, Guenther, and a two-year-old girl in 1953. My brother, Manfred, had come over with Elsbeth and Guenther. Next were my oldest sister Traute, her husband, Herbert, and their eleven-year-old son. Fritz came with his wife Renate in 1957. By the time I came in 1959, they had a daughter and a new baby boy.

My mother and father stayed behind because my grandmother, Papa's mother, was living with them. Another reason was my father's health. Papa worked in the coal mines for many years and by then suffered from black lung disease. He had to fight a lot of red tape with the immigration bureau. The authorities on both sides of the ocean wanted to make sure that immigrants were not a burden to society. First of all, one needed a sponsor to come over. Second, it was helpful when a person was young and healthy and able to work.

I stayed with my brother for about three months. My second-oldest sister, Elsbeth, and her husband came in May to pick me up. After our initial greetings, my sister looked me over. "Well, we did not know each other as children, now we have to get to know each other as adults."

Strange, but true. How well did we know each other? She was born in 1927. I was born in 1939. I had no idea what she experienced growing up.

The driving time from New Jersey to Michigan took about thirteen hours. We had ample time to start filling the voids in our mutual knowledge.

I started by saying, "You know, I don't remember you being home very much during the war."

"I can explain that," she said. "I was not home much from the time you turned two years until after the war."

"Why? Where were you?" I asked.

"I know you were only a baby, but do you know that all teenage girls at the time had to do one year of *Pflichtjahr*?" (Literally *compulsory year* — a sort of tour of duty.)

"Yes, Mama told me that was Hitler's way of training the German girls to be proficient in all aspects of housework. She also explained that you, Traute, and Frieda had to fulfill this requirement before you could start your careers."

Uh-hu, Elsbeth nodded her head in agreement, then proceeded with her *Pflichtjahr* experience. "I finished my eight years of school in 1941. Now I had to decide — either go to higher education or choose a trade. I wanted to be a secretary, but before I could start my apprenticeship, I had to do what was prescribed by the government. Everybody had to do this. It did not matter what the social standing of the youngster was. Rich or poor, farmer or city dweller, everybody had to do one year of labor service."

"We had a choice to either work on a farm or in a household with several children. These were jobs that nobody wanted and the pay was very low. The farms in Germany were mostly mixed farms, with work in the fields, in the household, or with the animals. But you did whatever needed to be done, and you did it when you were told to do it."

"Bigger farms had horses, cows, pigs, chickens, and geese. Most houses were *Fachwerkhäuser* (framework houses). These are half-timbered houses with plaster over stones and wooden beams going diagonally from one side to the other. You can see them all over Germany. Since I grew up in a city, I thought it would be nice to work on a farm. Once a person made the decision whether to go to a household with children or to work on a farm, she was told by the local government which farmer to go to. The farmer I was assigned to was not the largest but the richest in the area. They had a brick house and horses, while smaller farms had only cows. Oh yes, he also had two cows, but unfortunately, the couple had no children."

"Work was not always easy, but since it was a requirement, there was no use complaining. I made the best of it until my time was up and I was free to pursue my career as a secretary."

I could tell by the tone in Elsbeth's voice that she did not like what the government ordered for the young girls. For the first time, I wondered how it felt to live under a totalitarian government.

"Secretary?" I asked her. "Mama told me you wanted to be a nurse."

"That came later," she answered, "and that was another time I was away from home."

The more Elsbeth spoke, the more I understood why I didn't remember her during the earliest years of my life.

Then she continued. "I started my apprenticeship as a secretary at Krupp Steel Company in 1942. The company was in Essen, about twelve kilometers from Gelsenkirchen-Horst" (our hometown). "At the time, most people took public transportation to go to work. The streetcars were always full. Often people stood on the steps of the streetcar and held onto the handlebar. Safety rules were not enforced that much, because this was the middle of the war—the whole atmosphere was chaotic."

My sister grew more animated as the story went on. "I stayed at Krupp until 1944. The bombing was really getting intense. As a matter of fact, I knew every shelter on the way to Essen, because sometimes we had to seek shelter when there was a sudden air strike. During one of those air strikes, Krupp was hit and suffered major damage. As a result, I lost my job."

Krupp was a major weapon manufacturer in Germany. I even had a book about the Krupp family, *The Arms of Krupp*.

> In the Middle Ages, when Germany was weak, the Krupps appeared and plied their trade modestly in the walled city of Essen. During the Napoleonic era, when the country felt servile, the head of the house donned a French cockade and became a Francophile. Then, in the next half-century, Germany rose. The drums of conquest rolled in 1870, 1914, and 1939, and each time it was a Krupp who honed the Junker blade on the family's anvils. [1]

When Elsbeth lost her job in 1944 after the bombing of Krupp, it was the worst time to be unemployed. This was the fifth year of the war, and the infrastructure all over

---

[1] William Manchester, *The Arms of Krupp*, (New York: Bantam Books, Inc.)1

Germany was collapsing. My mother, Fritz, Manfred, and I were evacuated. Frieda was away from home doing her *Pflichtjahr*. Traute worked as a cook in a boys home.

Elsbeth finished her story. "When I lost my job, I found myself alone with Papa, who still worked in the coal mine. I thought the best thing to do was to join Traute in the boys home. They were operating on a shoestring budget and could not afford another worker, but they understood my situation and were willing to give me room and board for helping in the kitchen. Traute and I stayed there until the war was over."

Elsbeth leaned her head against the window—still in a reflective mood. The many hours driving to Michigan did not seem long at all. We arrived in Benton Harbor, the town where Elsbeth and Guenther had their first home.

I looked forward to getting reacquainted with my other siblings.

Chapter 2
Siblings Reunion in Michigan

I moved in with my brother Manfred. Because we were only three years apart, we spent the most time together as brother and sister while growing up. Manfred married a year before I came over. My new sister-in-law, Christa, also came from a German family

Growing up, Manfred and I played well together. We were together through all the war years. When the fighting grew severe, women and small children were evacuated to the countryside. Now I had a chance to reconnect with him and to get to know my new sister-in-law.

My twentieth birthday came up fast after I came from New Jersey. My three sisters and my brother gave me a big party. We were all excited, since we were separated for so many years.

As we sat around the dinner table, everybody wanted to share something of our past. My sisters talked about the time before I was born. Mama related many stories from the past, but now was the time to hear how my sisters felt about the earlier years.

The time between 1923, when my parents were married, and 1939, when I was born, were tumultuous years, even before the war started. The stories went from the personal to the political—back and forth. Growing up between two world wars, as my sisters did, one definitely could not have ignored the political background. Elsbeth talked lot about the political situation, so I'll let her tell us what she remembers.

Elsbeth

World War I ended in November 1918. France still occupied Germany, and according to my mother, life in Germany was very difficult. The political situation really deteriorated. Various political parties led demonstrations and riots. Each party claimed to have the solution for a better living standard.

Many people complained about the war reparations Germany had to pay to France. Dad was working in the coal mine. He made good money, but as the economy worsened and inflation increased, his earnings had less and less purchasing power. At first, he was making one thousand marks per month. In a short time, it grew to one million marks a month. This is hilarious! Can I actually say we were millionaires?

Then the food supply got very limited. To get the most available groceries, housewives waited at the gates of the mines grab their husbands' pay and run to the grocery store before the merchants ran out of stock. It was heartbreaking when some men went to the bar first, instead of going home. That meant the family wound up with less money to spend on food. It was at this terrible time that Papa lost his job.

"Anybody want another cup of coffee?" Traute interrupted.

"I think us guys should play a game of cards." Herbert looked expectantly at my brother Manfred and Guenther and Helmut, my other two brothers-in-law.

"I'm in," answered Manfred.

"I don't know about cards, but I will join you guys in the living room," said Guenther.

After everybody settled down, Traute took over as the speaker. She was the oldest and remembered the most about the early family life.

Traute

Papa's unemployment made life very difficult. Mother told me that sometimes she just did not know where the next meal would come from, or that she didn't have enough clothing for everybody. I must admire her, though, because she came up with creative ways to keep the household running smoothly. For example, merchants at the time used stamps that customers received when they did their shopping. For a certain number of stamps, the consumer received free merchandise. Sometimes Mother said, "Traute, count out the stamps and see if we have enough to get some groceries."

The stamps were not enough for a lot of groceries, but maybe just something to tie us over until the next unemployment benefit check came. One of the items I remember was the *Erbswurst*, instant pea soup made to look like a sausage.

While I was going to the store to purchase the *Erbswurst*, Mother put water in a pot, added an onion, potatoes, and spices. When I came home, she added the *Erbswurst* and that was our evening meal. Of course, there was no meat in it. Mother was happy if she had a little lard to enhance the flavor. We usually ate the soup with a slice of rye bread.

Papa also had very clever ideas about how to supply food for the family. We always had a garden for growing vegetables and fruit. The fruit included sour cherries, strawberries, currants, and gooseberries.

Vegetables included carrots, lettuce, kale, red beets, spinach, white and red cabbage, and potatoes. From the white cabbage, we made our own sauerkraut—a good provision for the winter months. We also stored potatoes in our basement.

When I think of our garden, I also remember the flowers. We had asters and a row of Lilies of the Valley growing along the hedge. They were among the first flowers to bloom in the springtime. Their little while bells amongst the dark green leaves were magnificent in their simplicity. In the far corner of the garden we had a white lilac tree, while our neighbor had a purple lilac tree. When both were in bloom, the air was filled with their beautiful fragrance.

Papa also kept some small domestic animals, like chickens and ducks, which gave us eggs, and goats that provided milk.

Sometimes the goats had kids—they were as cute as can be. When the weather was too cold for them to be in the stable, we brought them into the house. We put old rags in a corner of the kitchen and let them sleep right there.

When the goats were old enough to be sold, it was very hard to let them go, but Papa explained that we needed the money. We always kept at least one goat for the milk and eventually bought a churn to make our own butter.

As time went on, and Papa was still unemployed, he also bought a pig. The upkeep of all the animals and the garden was a lot of work, and since I was the oldest child, I had to help out a lot. Mother worked hard, but shortly after Fritz was born, she had a miscarriage, which left her weak and fatigued. My grandmother came sometimes to help, but it takes a lot of work to raise a family with four children under ten years old.

I was nine years old, going on ten. It was my job to take the goats to a meadow for feeding, after I came home from school. I often went to the Emscher River embankment where the grass was plentiful. I just sat there and did my homework or read, while the goats munched away on the luscious grass. In the late afternoon, it was time for the goats to be milked, so I grabbed the leash and led them back home.

Looking back now, it was not as bad as I perceived it to be when I was a child. Back then, I did not like walking the goats, because the kids in our neighborhood made fun of me and called me "goat-mother." Children can be cruel and being the recipient of teasing can hurt. Well, I guess I survived it unscathed.

I was not the only one who endured teasing on account of the goats. Mother told me that she was sometimes hurt by the remarks of one of my uncles. Whenever there was a birthday in our family, aunts, uncles, and cousins came together to celebrate. It was never a big party, just the family getting together for a kaffeeklatsch.

Since we lived in economically hard times, mother used the milk and butter from our goats to bake a cake. At the party, one of my uncles asked my mother, "Well, Anna, did you use goat milk or butter to make the cake?"

Of course she did! What did he expect from a family with an unemployed head of the household? So Mother said, "Yes, I used goat butter."

Then he answered, "Then I am not going to have any."

Oh, the insensibility of some people!

Besides taking the goats to the meadow, I also had to help find feed for the pig. Every night after dinner, my parents sent me to the neighbors to ask for table scraps. The table scraps were kept in a clay pot until there was enough that it could be mixed with some grain and fed to the pig. When the pig was slaughtered, we rewarded the neighbors with some sausage.

Slaughtering the pig gave us a good supply of meat. Papa did not slaughter our pigs—we hired a professional butcher for that. There were no freezers or refrigerators at the time in Germany. Mother canned most of the meat to preserve it. Papa built a smokehouse in which we hung up portions of meat that were suitable for smoking.

Frieda

I liked the way we celebrated everybody's birthdays. Mother always managed to bake a cake or two, even when we were short on provision. We did not have many other sweets, so a piece of cake was a nice treat.

Our relatives, mostly on my father's side, came for the party. If the birthday was for one of us children, we received a small gift. If it was an adult's birthday, a bouquet of flowers would suffice. Nobody had a lot of money, but we enjoyed each other's company, including all the cousins who came along. We had a wonderful time playing together.

But what really stands out in my memory is the singing. After we had the cake, Papa would get his table zither out and play our favorite hymns. Not all of our relatives attended the same church as we did, but they enjoyed singing along, regardless.

Mother and Papa, his brother Herman and his wife Liese, had beautiful voices. They often sang as a quartet in our church. Uncle Herman was not only a good singer, but also our Sunday school teacher, until he was drafted into the Wehrmacht (army) when the war started.

I want to tell you something that hurts a little even now as I look back to the early- to mid-thirties. When Hitler came into power, he encouraged families to have lots of children. In our neighborhood, there were quite a few families with five, six, or even seven children. Even though Hitler made a lot of promises for a better future, the economy took a long time to recover. In the meantime, families struggled to make ends meet. Many children suffered from malnutrition. Then the government took action by sending the children from poor families to *Erholungsheime* (recovery homes). These homes were established for the sole purpose of giving the children better nourishment, even if it was only for a short time.

I was sent away twice. The first time, I was only six years old. I stayed at the *Erholungsheim* for four weeks. The second time I was sent away, Fritz was to accompany me. I was seven years old and Fritz was six. We were sad and very homesick. We consoled each other by remembering and talking about what we liked at home. I told Fritz how I liked to sit in the back of Papa's bicycle and take a ride with him.

Sometimes, Papa took one child on the back seat and one child on the bar in front of him. Talking to each other like that made the time a little bit more bearable. However, we always were glad to go home again.

Helga

It seems to me that less food served with love and good company is better than plenty of food in a lonely place.

We were getting tired and decided to quit for the night.

Christa, our new sister-in-law, spoke up. "This is really fascinating. I am looking forward to hearing more about your past."

We set a date for just the women of the family to get together to go down memory lane.

The front and back of the Mother Cross

Chapter 3
Ladies' Luncheon

Helga

We met at Traute's house again. Entertaining people was Traute's specialty. She just loved to have company. She served us a homemade German potato salad with frankfurters. For desert, she had a fresh fruit torte.

"So, where did we leave off the last time we talked?" Traute asked.

"I'd like to hear more about the political atmosphere," I said.

Traute looked at Elsbeth. "You're good at that. Want to start?"

"Okay," Elsbeth answered. "I'll tell you more about life before the war."

Elsbeth

Politically speaking, the times were very tumultuous. All the political parties tried to get the majority of people on their side. Hitler with his fascist party won the election in 1933. It is hard to believe, knowing what we now know, but Hitler promised people jobs and a better life. The beginning was indeed hopeful. Law and order was established and jobs were created. Hitler's government came up with a four-year plan to build up the German infrastructure. This included building a better highway system. Hence, Germany's famous autobahn came into being. Maybe Hitler thought that would be good for military transport.

Hitler also had a vision for every German family to own a home and drive a little Volkswagen. To make it easier for people to accomplish this, he started what was called *Bauverein* (building co-ops). People were encouraged to lay aside a little money every month. When their account reached a certain amount, the family could get a loan with a very low interest rate to start building their home.

These actions pushed the unemployment rate down tremendously, but there were still people who did not find jobs. However, everybody had to work. Whoever lacked a job had to report to a predetermined place early in the morning, from where they were transported by buses to parks and highways. There they had to do whatever was necessary: cut the grass, collect the litter, rake the walkways in the park, and so on. In the evening, they were brought back and received money for the day's work. Of course, these were minimum-wage jobs, but who did not work, did not get paid. No free unemployment money!

Traute

I remember that the general mood among the population changed from a sigh of relief to contemplating what lay ahead for the future. As Elsbeth related to us, there was a lot of road construction, but there were also factories for energy production. In our small town of Gelsenkirchen-Horst, the Gelsenberg Mining Corporation build the Gelsenberg-Benzin AG.

This plant produced gasoline mainly used in airplanes (perhaps for the future Luftwaffe?). I do not know if it was for safety or security, but the owners of the gasoline plant built a stone wall all around the plant. It reached all the way to our house. That meant they took away land that was used for gardens behind our house and others. To have your own garden was a huge economic help for the residents. The factory administrators realized this and knew it was not good public relations to take the land away. So they allowed the people to use a piece of land by the Emscher River that was part of their property.

Naturally, we took advantage of it. Papa planted the most stable vegetables used in the German diet: potatoes, cabbage, kale, spinach, and carrots. After we had the pig, Papa also planted *Runkeln*, a root vegetable similar to a turnip but mainly used for feed.

Helga

In 1936, our brother Manfred was born. Now there were five children in the Lenk family. Since Hitler liked large families, he awarded a Mother Cross to every woman after her fifth child was born. So Mother received her award. To honor my parents, I have to establish that they did not care what the government thought about large families. My parents believed that children are a gift from God.

Over the radio and in newspapers, there was more and more fascist propaganda. Hitler's speeches were enthusiastic about Germany's golden future—the Third Reich! However, soon the speeches included complaints that there was not enough land for the inhabitants. Men were recruited into military service, and schoolteachers were instructed to teach the children to be patriotic.

Traute asked Elsbeth," Do you want to start talking about our experiences during our school years?"

"Yes, I will," she said.

Elsbeth

The first thing that comes to mind is that our classes were very large. Sometimes we had up to sixty children in one class. The teachers were strict disciplinarians. If boys misbehaved, they got a spanking on their behind. If girls misbehaved, they had to stretch their hands out. The teacher would then administer one or two lashes with a bamboo stick.

Before classes started, we had to line up in the schoolyard according to the grade we were in. The flag was raised and we sang the National Anthem, *"Deutschland, Deutschland über alles."* After that we sang, *"Die Fahne hoch, die Reihen sind geschlossen ..."* (raise the flag high, stand orderly in your ranks ...) a typical marching song with a Nazi slogan. We had to raise our right arm and hold it up the whole time we were singing. I remember my arm got so tired that I put it on the person in front of me (we all did).

At that time the schools were separated by religion. We went to a Lutheran school. The Catholic school was right next to ours. There was a brick wall with an iron fence separating the two schools. There was no friendship among us. On the contrary, we threw little stones at each other. There was such animosity between the religions that even marriages between Catholics and Lutherans were frowned on.

Traute interrupted. "I remember what you called Lutheran school was really the state school. There were only two kind of schools in our district: one Catholic and the others for everybody else. You could say it was a state school."

"Well, I guess you are right," Elsbeth said. "Why don't you tell us your side of our school years?"

Traute

The schools were very far from our house. Classes started at eight o'clock in the morning, so we had to get up early. There were no school buses. We walked twenty-five to thirty minutes to get there. The schools were quite primitive compared to today's standards. Ours had only eight classrooms. The heat in the rooms was provided by a big pot-bellied stove. The janitor had to start very early in the morning to get the coals hot and glowing. The stove was big enough to keep the coal burning for hours. Only on extremely cold days was it necessary for the maintenance man to come back and add more coals.

Elsbeth mentioned the classes were all big. There were too many children in the grade I was in. The teacher had a very difficult time, because it was hard to keep the kids focused on the lesson. To remedy the situation, the teacher moved some kids out of the class. Unfortunately, I was among the kids she appointed to go to a different school. This new school was in the area where my parents had their first apartment. In the meantime, we had moved, and the school was pretty far away from our new home. I was unhappy about the situation. I was also mad, because now I had to get up at seven o'clock in the morning to be on time. It was especially difficult in the winter months when it was dark and cold. Even worse—we had to pass a cemetery and a wooded area. There were no houses nearby. I was scared and felt lonely.

After a year, it happened that this school also grew overfilled. I was moved to yet another school. However, I was in my last year and that made it a little easier, because the end was in sight. With all the moves from one school to another, it was hard to make new friends. It frustrated me, because as soon as I found some friends, I was transferred again.

Well, I should tell you, there was a silver lining in the last transfer, though. Oma (our grandmother) lived close to where the new school was, and she always told me, "Trautchen (that is what she called me), why don't you stay with me at least one night per week, that saves you getting up so early every morning."

I took advantage of her offer. Oma lived in an apartment on the third floor in a three-story house. There were two apartments on each floor. It was a custom that the tenants took turns cleaning the stairwell once a week. So I stayed with her every Friday night and cleaned the stairwell on Saturdays.

Grandma's apartment was small but cozy. She decorated it nicely with hand-crocheted doilies on the furniture and live plants on the windowsill. Oma loved to have me over. She made a special effort to cook something I liked—potato pancakes, or some other dish she knew I would appreciate. It was a memorable time when we sat down at the dinner table to eat our meal. We conversed easily together, so it was an enjoyable time for both of us.

Come to think of it, I was the first grandchild from her son Ferdinant. Mother had two miscarriages before I was born, so the parents were very grateful when the third pregnancy resulted in a baby.

"I am not saying that Oma did not love you"—she looked at Elsbeth and Frieda—"but you know how grandparents are with their first grandchild!"

"It's all right," Elsbeth said. "It's all a long time ago. Let me tell you more about Hitler's plans for the population."

Elsbeth

We already talked about Hitler wanting big families. He claimed that the children, as Germany's future, belonged to him. He gave special attention to gifted children by giving them the best education free of charge.

To make sure that the children followed his ideology, the government started all kinds of clubs and summer camps. There was the *Bund Deutscher Mädchen* (German Girl's Club) for teenage girls and the Hitler Youth for teenage boys. The summer camps were mainly for the younger kids. The organizers provided interesting activities, so kids were eager to join.

However, my parents realized this was a clever way to keep the children from being involved in church life. It was a tricky situation, because the authorities did not tell the kids not to go to church; but the club's activities were on Sunday mornings and the children were expected to attend. Our parents, who attended church on a regular basis, did not like that at all.

Another thing the parents didn't like was that the government had the audacity to change the name of our beloved Christmas to "Winter Solstice Day." The governing authorities were more and more infringing on people's lives. Soon there was fear throughout the populace. It seemed everybody was suspicious of their own neighbor. We heard that people were arrested for "political" reasons. We wondered what they meant by *political*.

Questions and uncertainty about what was going on were the topics around many family dinner tables.

As the economy began to improve, Hitler started to build his military system. Every boy who turned eighteen years old had to go for one year of military training. By the time the population had reached eighty million, Hitler saw his opportunity. His new slogan was "We are a people without a land." That was his way of preparing the people for war: know the problem and be on his side for the solution.

Another proposal was to get back the lands Germany lost after WWI. Families who lived in these border countries belonged now to this and then to that country. Some people were upset. Traditional people liked to have their own identity: Austrian, French, Polish, or German—others were impartial. It did not take long, after the many ardent speeches Hitler is known for, to annex Austria, the Czech Republic, and Alsace, thereby carrying out his promises.

One of Hitler's strange ideas (now well known), was to have a pure race. No mixed marriages of any kind were allowed. His goal was to have an all-Aryan race which, to the Nazi way of thinking, meant Caucasian, but not of Jewish descent. Mostly blond, blue-eyed people.

Hitler was prejudiced against Jews and wanted Germany to be "cleaned" of them. It started with the infamous *Kristallnacht* in November 1938. Jewish people were taken out of their homes and brought to the train station for further transportation. The synagogues were set on fire, and Jewish businesses were plundered and demolished. Hence the name *Kristallnacht* (literally crystal night), because of all the broken storefront windows.

To be fair, I should include that Hitler gave Jewish people an opportunity to leave the country, if they chose to do so—at least up to a set date. Many took advantage of it, while others liked living in Germany and did not want to leave their homeland.

We had two Jewish families in our congregation who had converted to Christianity. They left Germany while the time allowed it. One moved to Brazil, the other to Argentina.

The Jews who decided to stay had to wear a Star of David on their outer clothing. We had Jewish friends and neighbors. We had shopped in their stores and could not understand what was happening.

Rumors spread that the Jews were put in labor camps. The slogan written over the entrance to the concentration camp at Dachau reads *Arbeit Macht Frei* (Work Brings Freedom).

It was a lot easier for the general public to believe that people were brought to labor camps than to concentration camps. However, as far as I know, there is not a German living today who does not feel some national guilt.

Chapter 4
The Beginning of the Conflict

Elsbeth

The war started about one year after *Kristallnacht*. I was twelve years old and remember the time very well. I can almost for certain say the day of the week. That can be explained very easily: every Thursday and Friday there was a farmer's market in our town. In actuality it was a combination farmer's and flea market. The merchandise, however, was all new. It was a wonderful cacophony of farmers, odds-and-ends housewares merchants, artisans, and fish mongers. The booths were organized by the kind of merchandise being offered. At times it got very noisy, because the merchants would call out their current specials to attract customers.

The market was on the town square, about a fifteen-minute walk from our house.

At that time we had no televisions, and the radio programs were not very entertaining, so it was a custom for people to lean on their windowsills and watch the pedestrians go by. On this particular day people shouted from their windows, "Have you heard the latest news? Hitler is mobilizing—we are going to war!"

It was a fact. Eligible men were called up in the middle of the night, and all young men eighteen years of age and up had to report to a military post. The reaction among the population varied. Some were crying, some were laughing, and still others had a foreboding fear.

Many were old enough to remember WWI and did not want another war, either because they had lost a loved one or knew of soldiers who were missing in action and nobody knew what happened to them. Unfortunately, Hitler also had followers who were eager to turn Germany into a world power.

The war was started by Germany invading Poland. Ironically, British, French, and German diplomats had negotiated for months prior to the Polish invasion to ensure that peace prevailed in Europe. The British and French ambassadors had warned the Germans that they would stand with Poland should Hitler try to capture the territories he claimed belonged to Germany. However, Hitler's generals felt confident that they were bluffing.

The fact remains—Hitler's Wehrmacht invaded Poland. Britain and France reluctantly entered the war. Soon the German Luftwaffe and the British Air Force were conducting air raids over each other's countries.

We lived in a highly industrial part of Germany and therefore became a steady target. Our town of Gelsenkirchen-Horst had the largest gas production facility in the world. Our parents told us that they were trained on how to use a gas mask, in case the gasometer were hit by a bomb. It actually was hit once, but the damage was only minor.

Bomb shelters were just being built, so in the beginning of the war we sought shelter in our basements. Eventually a bomb shelter was built across from our house. That's where we had to go to during an air raid. The bunker was six stories high, and the walls were one meter thick, constructed of concrete reinforced by steel rods. The roof was about one and a half meters thick. This all gave us a sense of safety.

City officials gave us instruction on the sound of the alarms. There were three alarms given before an air strike. The first alarm sounded when the enemy planes were detected and the second when they approached our city. The third, an acute alarm, signaled the time everybody had to be in the bunker. We had to stay in the bunker until we heard one long sound, indicating it was safe to go home. By that time, we missed half a night's sleep.

Starting around 1941, the air raids came almost every night. Sometimes, we did not bother to go to bed anymore. At nine o'clock in the evening we took our little suitcases and went into the bunker until two or three o'clock in the morning. Life grew more and more dangerous.

While the men went to war, the women took over many factory jobs. A lot of workers were needed in the ammunition factories and in the field of communication. Telephone operators and typists were needed to process fast incoming news.

After I finished my *Pflichtjahr*, I started my apprenticeship at The Krupp Steel Company.

Chapter 5
Born in Germany in 1939

Helga

Can a person's date of birth have a special legacy? I am thinking of George Orwell's novel *1984* or the movie *Born on the Fourth of July*.

Can I ignore the historical fact that my birth year coincided with the beginning of the biggest war in the twentieth century? Hardly! The earliest memories of my childhood are filled with sounds of sirens, confused and scared people running to shelters, and a general atmosphere of chaos.

That is the historical background, and I have lots more to say about that. First, I'd like to share events on a personal level.

Mama liked the fact that I was a girl. Mother was thirty-eight years old when I was born and she thought *If this is the last child, I want it to be a girl, so she can help me in my golden years.*

My father wanted a boy, because so far there were three girls and two boys. So he said, "If it is a boy, we have three pairs."

Well, Mama received her first wish, but as far as taking care of her in her golden years, that fell to my sister Elsbeth—thank you, Elsbeth!

During one of the many talks I had with my mother growing up, she related the circumstances of my birth. At that time most children were born at home with the help of a midwife. My birth was expected during the first week in July. My grandmother, who usually came to stay with us whenever Mama had another baby, was out of town on vacation. Since ordinary citizens did not have telephones, they could not notify Grandmother when Mama started her labor pains.

Mother called Elsbeth to fetch the midwife and told Traute to stay with her. This was at the end of June, several days earlier than expected. So all the things Grandmother would have done, Traute had to do. She washed the linens, cooked the meals for the family, and took care of her younger siblings. It still amazes me as I write this—Traute was only fourteen years old at the time!

When Grandma finally arrived from her vacation, she exclaimed, "My, the baby is here already! How did you manage?"

"Well, Traute did everything," Mother answered. "She even washed the diapers on a washboard." Disposable diapers were unheard of at the time.

Shortly after my birth, Mama suffered from varicose veins inflammation. It was rather severe, and she had to be hospitalized. Mama told me that since she was still nursing me, she took me along to the hospital. The hospital staff put me in the children's section, while she was one floor above in the women's section. When it was time for my feeding, a nurse would bring me to her. However, I did not sleep through the night yet, so the nurses brought me late at night and then early in the morning. Mama said she heard me cry during the night.

She really could not have heard me, but I guess she worried that I might be hungry.

After both of us went home, she said my belly button was all bandaged up. So she thought I probably did cry! Well, forced sleeping through the night didn't cause any harm to me and probably gave Mother more rest.

Another story connected with the hospital was that my grandfather was in the hospital at the same time. He suffered from kidney stones. Unfortunately, he passed away while Mother and I were still in the hospital. This meant that my mother could not attend her father's funeral.

Life can be hard.

I believe I can trace my earliest memory to 1942, when I was three years old going on four. It was a terrible night. I have some recollection of standing in our backyard holding Traute's hand while watching a fire from afar. It must have been cold, because I also remember wearing white mittens with a red star on the back of the hands. As we walked back to the front entrance, I let my hand slide along the ledge on the wall. It made the inside hand of the mitten totally black in minutes. After all, we lived in close proximity to a coal mine. Everything was covered with a fine layer of dust. If I try to analyze why I remember details like that, I could only guess that those mittens were new and meant a lot to me. I thought they were ruined.

Traute remembers that night better than I.

Traute

I remember one particular air strike while I was still at home. It was a Saturday, which meant it was a bath day. This may sound weird at the present time, but at that time in Germany, we took a bath only once a week. Since we had only cold running water, we carried the cold water in buckets to the kitchen, where we put our galvanized bath tub, and heated up some water on the kitchen stove.

Mother had just finished giving Helga and Manfred their bath, when all of a sudden, we heard bombs falling and shots being fired. We could not believe it! Did we miss the alarm? Now it was too late to run to the shelter.

The best thing we could do was to huddle together under the stairs that led to the second floor. It was very noisy outside. We heard airplanes and bombs falling. The blasts from exploding bombs ripped the shutters of our kitchen window off their hinges. They landed on the floor with a loud bang.

When I heard a crackling sound, I sneaked to the window to see what was going on. "Oh my, oh my" I cried. "Mother, the whole *Industrie Strasse* is burning!"

My aunt, Anna, lived around the corner from our house on the street that was engulfed in flames. I wanted to go outside immediately to watch the fire, but Papa told me to wait for the siren to announce that the air strike was over.

People coming out of the bunker were guided by the police on a detour away from the burning buildings. Since we were home, I ran around the corner to see if my aunt's house had been hit.

The fire trucks with their men were working hard to extinguish the flames. They were too engrossed in their work to pay attention to me. My aunt's house was burning on one side only. Aunt Anna was not home, and I wondered if I could salvage something before the fire reached the other side. I saw a ladder leaning against the wall. I quickly got it and put it up under Aunt Anna's window.

I managed to climb through the window to see what I could save for her. Despite the danger, something made me laugh. There was cake dough on the table, obviously made with yeast and left to rise. Well rise it did! It was totally out of proportion from all the heat in the air.

A picture of my cousin, Willy—already an early casualty of the war—hung on the wall above the sofa. I made my way to the living room, snatched the photo off the wall, and hurried back out. I guess I did all this without thinking.

Now panic set in. I fled as fast as I could, but I felt good, because I thought at least she would have a picture of Willy as a souvenir.

This all happened during the night. When morning came, we were able to see all the damage from this attack. A bomb had fallen right in our garden and left a big crater. The area was blocked off and the police told us to stay in the house. The bomb squad wanted to be sure that there was not another bomb that needed to be defused. This actually happened a lot. Sometimes people had to wait to go home until the authorities had made a thorough check of the neighborhood.

I was away from home for several years during the war, but this was one time I was home. This was also the time I fell deeply in love.

Chapter 6

A Love Story

Helga

It was 1942 when Traute fell in love with a soldier. A division of the Wehrmacht called flak (*Flugabwehrkanone,* that is, antiaircraft guns) was stationed in our town. I can surmise that it was because of the Gelsenberg-Bezine AG gas refinery and all the coal mines. We needed to have a good defense in place. Herbert was born in Austria, but after the Anschluss (annexation) of Austria, all qualified men were incorporated into the German Wehrmacht. So it happened that Herbert was serving in the flak in Gelsenkirchen.

Traute

Our cousin, Willy Braun—whom I mentioned earlier when I rescued his photo from my aunt's house—had been engaged to a girl named Martha. Since he was killed in action, Martha was going around with a sad expression on her face. Who could blame her? Of course she missed him.

Grandma was a very observant person. One Sunday afternoon she said to me, "Trautchen, why don't you go to Martha and spend some time with her. Cheer her up a little bit."

"Ja, I think that would be a good idea," I answered.

So I went to Martha's house and said, "Let's go out for a while."

Martha was glad for the invitation, and the two of us proceeded to a farmhouse that had been turned into a country eatery serving coffee, cakes, and small snacks. I heard that families liked to go there, because it was outside the town and had a sandbox and a swing set for the children.

I even remember the dress I wore. It was a nice shade of lilac, and I wore a gray hat with it. People used to dress up on Sundays, and we were proud of our outfits.

I had not been to this place before, so when we entered the dining room, I was shocked. There were hardly any families, as I thought there would be, but a lot of soldiers. I did not know what we should do, but Martha said, "Oh come on, let's stay and have a cup of coffee."

At one table, six soldiers sat engrossed in a card game, but they did look up as we settled down at the table next to them. Pretty soon one of the soldiers started flirting with Martha. Then he and another one (Herbert) asked if they could join us at our table.

We nodded, giving them permission. I looked at Herbert and thought, *he sure is handsome!* He had black wavy hair and blue eyes. What a nice contrast!

Our conversation flowed freely. The afternoon flew by, and the time came for the soldiers to return to duty. Before they departed, they asked us if we would come back next Sunday. We didn't commit ourselves right away, but said we would think about it. All the way home we giggled as we talked about the looks of the soldiers and how nice they were.

Martha and I talked during the week, and we decided to go back the following Sunday. It did not take long for this to become routine. To be honest with myself, I realized I was falling in love with Herbert.

Mother became a little suspicious. She actually checked my handbag. In it she found the address from Herbert that I had written on a piece of paper. Mother was very upset, because I was already writing to ten soldiers. She confronted me. "Are ten soldiers not enough? To how many do you want to write to?"

Defensively I said, "Mother, I am not in love with any of them. I only write because people encourage girls to write letters to soldiers. Some of those boys are my former classmates, you know that!"

Mother was not convinced. She took the piece of paper with the address from Herbert and threw it into the fire. I can still see her in my mind, holding the top ring of the front burner as she threw the paper into the flames. (An explanation for the younger readers: On a coal-burning stove one could remove rings from a burner to adjust the desired heat).

I was still angry. "I don't need his address. I can still visit him where he is stationed." Suddenly I thought *What if she grounds me?* So I tried a softer approach. "What if I stop writing to all the other ones? Herbert may be sent to another city."

"That's even worse," Mama said. "Soldiers have a new girlfriend in every city they go to. You might as well forget about him."

Herbert occupied my thoughts more and more. How could I forget about him?

As it happened, Herbert did get orders to be transferred. It was not just another city, it was another country. His military unit was transported to the front in France. Herbert told me he loved me and did not want to lose me. He wanted to come back to Gelsenkirchen as soon as he could or when the war was over. So Herbert asked my parents for permission to get engaged.

My parents were not thrilled about it. Mother tried to reason with me. "You are only seventeen years old. You should be a model for your younger sisters. How would you feel if they follow your example?"

Papa said similar things as Mama had said before. "Most soldiers are not faithful; don't you know that? Herbert will forget about you in France."

After more warning words, the parents finally consented. We celebrated our engagement before Herbert left for France.

Bunker stands as a memorial

Chapter 7
Four Years of Intense War

Helga

Airstrikes constantly reminded us how close to home the war was. We lived right in the midst of it. If you consider that I experienced all the accompanying horrors of the war before my sixth birthday, it is no wonder that the memory of it is permanently embedded in my mind.

Starting from the fall of 1941, the airstrikes came almost every night. We were fortunate that we had a bomb shelter diagonally across from our house. It just took us a few minutes to get there. The bunker was a square building like a gigantic cement block. However, the architecture was enhanced by red bricks on the outside walls. This gave the building extra strength, as well as a classical German look.

There were no windows, only small openings, approximately two by four feet with an iron door that could be opened for fresh air.

Traute and Elsbeth talked about the sounding of the alarm. Since the enemy attacks came mainly during the night, every house had to be totally dark. We had to hang up blackout curtains on all the windows. This was strictly enforced by the local police. This police force consisted mainly of men who were too old or otherwise not capable to fight in combat.

We all had our little suitcases and grabbed them at the sound of the first siren. I honestly do not know what was in those suitcases, but I can imagine it was some valuables our parents wanted to save or extra clothing. The uncertainty of one's home was constantly on people's minds.

Even today I can still hear the sound of the alarm in my head. Most of us have heard it when watching a war movie. It is a long howling sound, penetrating the ear, and at times of war it invokes fear of things to come.

Even though the walls of the bunker where very thick, we still heard the bombs falling, especially when they exploded in the immediate neighborhood. The end of an airstrike was greeted with relief and anxiety. Relief because it was over, anxiety about what destruction had been caused by the bombs. As I mentioned earlier, some bombs did not detonate, so they had to be defused before people were allowed to return to their homes.

Many times streets were blocked off because of burning buildings. It was devastating when people were confronted with their residence burning or destroyed.

This happened to our neighbor. Their house was hit during one attack. We did not see it burning, but there was a big empty space with a hole in the floor where the living and dining rooms had been. The house looked like a shell. It was a duplex with a front porch holding two entrances. The porch and the common roof remained intact. The front and the sides of the house still stood, but its back was blown out.

The neighbor fixed up his tool shed and added space to it for them to use as a temporary shelter. The family in the other half of the building kept on living in it. Of course, no houses were rebuilt while the war was going on.

When I visited my hometown in 1970, most of the smaller homes had been replaced by multifamily apartment housing. In place of the gardens that people had when I was growing up, there was now a playground for all the children living in the apartments.

Waiting Out an Airstrike

Strange stories circulated inside the bunker during an airstrike. One such story was that a person didn't make it in time to enter the shelter and was hit in the middle of the street. His body parts were strewn all over the street and sidewalk.

Another one was that a woman stayed in her basement during an attack. Unfortunately, a bomb fell through her chimney and exploded.

Then there was a woman with gray hair on one of her cheeks. Rumor had it that she had seen a mouse in the bunker. The sight of it so frightened her that she instinctively raised her hand to her face, and that place under her hand now had gray hair like a mouse. I am not going to vouch for this one, but the first two are true.

One attack was so severe we had to stay in the bunker for three days. The bombs hit the steeple roof and totally destroyed it, but the rest of the building stood firm. However, the walls shook from the pressure and dust filled the air. This made breathing very difficult. Manfred and I were on the top bunk of the bed, where one of the openings in the walls was. The people asked Manfred to open the iron door for fresh air. That cleared up the air somewhat, but now we also heard more of the noise accompanying an air raid.

During those three days, only one family member was allowed to go home for a brief time for food. In our family it was Frieda, my sister who happened to be home at the time. Frieda is the sister whom I least remember. First, she had to do her *Pflichtjahr*, and then Mama, Fritz, Manfred and I were evacuated. Anyway, she went home to make some home-fried potatoes. To this day, I have a dislike of home-fried potatoes, including French fries.

I may be wrong, but I believe it goes back to that time, because most Germans are potato lovers. It's a staple. Mama would make it when an unexpected guest came to visit. Of course, at home she served it with fresh eggs from our own chickens.

One time a big commotion and excited talk rose among the neighbors. We soon found out that a Russian airplane had been shot down in the next village. Traute took me by the hand, and the two of us walked about a kilometer to where the plane went down.

The local civilian police tried to keep the people away, but we managed to get a look at the dead pilot on the ground. His eyes were staring into the sky and his mouth was wide open.

What a sight for a little kid.

Chapter 8
Evacuation and Airstrikes Away from Home

Helga

At times when the attacks were very severe, mothers with small children were sent away from the cities to the countryside, where the fighting was less intense. We were evacuated twice—one time to Bavaria and the other time to Stadtlohn, near the Holland border. The first time, we were a party of six. My mother, Manfred, myself, and my Aunt Hannah with her two children, Friedhelm and Erika. This was in the early part of the war, when Fritz was still in a boy's camp in Czechoslovakia (today's Slovakia).

The farmer we were sent to was in the greater Munich area. One night this beautiful city became the target of an airstrike. When it was over we all stood in the front yard and watched the night sky from a distance. The bombs hit their targets. Buildings burned, sending smoke and fiery sparks into the air.

A neighbor informed us that, among other buildings, a Catholic church was hit.

Some farmers got their horse-drawn carriages and hurried to the city to see if anything could be salvaged. The people offered their homes for storage. This is how the parlor of our host family became home of several statues of saints.

I was never in a Catholic church, so seeing these statues of saints was something new to me. The one I found particularly interesting was the Virgin Mary with a bleeding heart. Joseph, her earthly husband, was a sitting statue which now decorated the hallway to the barn adjoining the house. Unfortunately for me, the bathroom was in the barn. If I had to use the bathroom in the middle of the night, I had to pass the saints in the parlor and Joseph in the hallway. I believe I must have been a little frightened — why else would I remember all this in detail?

The farmers had no choice about taking us in. The governing authorities ordered farmers to take in mothers with small children from the industrial areas.

Of course, Mama had to help with the household chores. I recall seeing her doing a lot of ironing. Ironing was a cumbersome task at the time. First, there was no easy-care material. Second, the iron itself was very heavy. It was made of cast iron and had to be repeatedly heated up on the stove. There was another type of iron that was hollow and had two iron parts—one could be used while the other one was being heated.

Thinking back, not everything that happened was tragic. A funny thing happened on our way to Bavaria.

All of Europe is known for its great railroad system. When the order came for mothers and children to be evacuated, they had to report to the train station where they were told which part of Germany they would be sent to.

The trains were always crowded. I remember one time on a long trip my mother laid me into the cord-woven luggage basket above the seats. Thinking about those luggage baskets, I don't know if there was a way to strap me in. But I guess if it was safe for suitcases not to fall on people during the train ride, it was safe for me to be there.

I do not recall the duration of our time in Bavaria, but Mama told me that Manfred was old enough to start school. Since he was born in 1936, this must have been 1942, when he was six years old.

Mother asked the farmer if Manfred could go with his children. The parents agreed, but the children were very cruel. They constantly teased him saying, "You are a Prussian, we are *bures* (Bavarian for farmer), we do not want to walk with you."

It was hard on Manfred. Mama wanted to do the right thing, but also felt sorry for her little boy. She tried her best to be sympathetic, but made him go to school anyway—even if it meant he had to walk alone.

Once we were allowed to return home, he went to school in our hometown, even though the war was still raging. Then we were evacuated again.

With all this going from one place to another, Manfred had a little bit of first grade, some of second and third, but never completed a full grade. When the war was finally over, he was entered into fourth grade according to his age.

It was disastrous for him, because he had not mastered his basic math and now had to deal with higher math, like fractions.

Can one blame him for loathing learning? After he finished eighth grade, he did not even want to enter into an apprenticeship. In an apprenticeship, one still had to go to school one or two days a week. The alternative was to work in the coal mines, which was painful for my father to think about. Papa knew the consequences of working in the mines. Black lung disease is terrible, and Papa suffered immensely. He and Manfred had many arguments. Papa tried to argue that there are trades that don't require that much schooling, but Manfred did not want to hear of it.

In the end, Manfred entered employment at the coal mines, but not *unter Tage* (underground). Workers were not subjected to work underground until they were sixteen years old.

During those years of 1942–1945, each of my older sisters did her *Pflichtjahr*. Fritz was in several boy's camps. So it seems there was a lot of coming and going in our household. Papa was working as a coal miner again. He was exempt from serving in the Wehrmacht, because coal was the main source of energy.

A coal miner's job might have been one of the lowest available, but it worked out just fine for Papa. He did not agree with Hitler's ideology and was happy that he did not have to participate in all the things going on under the Hitler regime.

Chapter 9
Mother's Courage in the Face of Fascism

Helga

Hitler's totalitarian government seemed to infiltrate all phases of family life. I already shared the *Pflichtjahr* for girls. For boys, there was the Hitler Youth and for small children different camps. My brother Fritz was in several camps during the summer months. He enjoyed being there, because the leaders provided interesting things to do for the kids. The last camp Fritz went to was in Czechoslovakia. He was twelve years old going on thirteen.

By the end of the summer, the leader wanted to keep him, because in December of that year (1943), he would be thirteen, old enough to enter the Hitler Youth. However, in the fall, he became ill with tonsillitis. When Mama heard about it, she did not waste any time. She went to the camp immediately to bring her son home. My parents did not agree with the Nazi ideology, and the last thing they wanted was for the authorities to captivate Fritz's mind.

Of course, this meant that Mama had to confront the camp leaders, who were all too eager to do their part to influence the boys to fit the Nazi mold. I have profound respect for my mother for standing up to the leaders and demanding her rights as a parent of a minor.

Legally, they could not keep Fritz until he was thirteen. Amazing—some private rights still prevailed.

Mother traveled by train from Germany to Czechoslovakia. She told me that when she came to the camp and spoke with the administrators, they told her, "You cannot take your boy home. The youth of this country belong to the Fuehrer!"

But Mother was firm. Then the leader of Fritz's group told her, "There are consequences if you insist with your intentions. We will withhold the food coupon for Fritz."

As the war dragged on, food supplies were scarce. People could buy food only with coupons they received according to the number of persons in a household.

Mama did not budge at the pressure of this gestapo-type person. She told him this would not change her mind. She threw her response in his face. "The rest of the family will share their food with Fritz."

I am proud to announce that she won the battle. She took her boy home. I wonder if she remembered what went through her head when she was pregnant with Fritz, namely, *If this is going to be a boy, I will dedicate his life to the Lord.*

My father had a special secret. The regular greeting in Germany is *guten tag* or *guten abend* (good day or good evening), but at Hitler's time it was all "heil Hitler." It did not matter what time of the day it was, it was the same morning afternoon or evening. One could also say *"heil fuehrer"* (*fuehrer* is literally translated as leader—of any kind). Papa used to greet people with *"heil unser fuehrer"* (hail our leader, meaning Jesus Christ). This may be trivial in some people's eyes, but Papa knew his heart followed an eternal leader, rather than a temporal one.

This box is similar to the one I received

Chapter 10
Our Second Evacuation

Helga

The second time we were evacuated, it was to an area near the Holland border. There were no bomb shelters in this little village. I assume shelters were just in the bigger cities. How did people react in a case of an attack? If people were in their homes, they would go into their basements. If they were outside they would fling themselves into ditches along the country roads.

This happened once to Mother and me. I was lying with my head touching another girl's head. Unfortunately, this girl had lice. Needless to say, the lice found their way over to my head. When I started scratching my head a few days later, my mother was shocked by what she discovered.

Every morning she combed my hair with a very fine-toothed comb trying to comb out the invaders. Her tender loving care, however, was fruitless. Finally, she managed to buy a special shampoo that promised to get rid of lice. She washed my hair with this shampoo. It burned like crazy, but it did the job. Oh, what a relief!

Another time we were out in the fields—I believe Mother was helping with the harvest—when we heard planes approaching. There was a barn in the far corner of the field in which we sought shelter. Airstrikes could last for quite a while. Most of the time people tried to encourage each other when they realized others were scared. They also shared any food they might have had with them.

I have a fond memory from this time. Somebody gave me a half of a boiled goose egg. I was awed by the sheer size of it, never having seen a goose egg before. My tiny hands encircled the egg, while my eyes focused on the delicious looking yellow circle surrounded by the white. I was hungry and overwhelmed with thankfulness.

Two of my sisters, Traute and Frieda, were surprised once by an attack on their way home. They saw the bombs falling and heard loud artillery fire. They hid as best as they could. It was very dangerous to be caught outside away from shelters. Thank God, they were not harmed.

Away from the cities we experienced the war a little differently than at home. For example, the farmers liked to watch whenever parachutes were landing nearby. People were not afraid of American and British parachutists, because they came to help bringing about the end of the war. But if the soldiers did not take their parachutes with them, the farmers looked for them and took them home. It was very unlikely that soldiers would return to the same area, because they were on a mission. However, women liked the parachute material and found a way to make blouses out of it.

As the war went on for several years, it became obvious to most people that Germany was fighting a losing battle. But suddenly there was talk of new hope in the air. The reason for this hope was that ammunition manufacturers developed a new weapon. I am talking about the first rockets—V1 and V2. This was supposed to turn the tide in Germany's favor.

When I transport myself to that time, the mental picture in my mind is of a lightning flash. The rockets lit up the sky in a brilliant color, much like shining gold. We could observe them from the little town by the Dutch border, flying high in the sky toward England. Adults could even distinguish by the sound and the pattern they flew which missile it was. On spotting them, they would shout, "Look, there is a V1" or "—a V2."

As I write this, I think it is quite remarkable the unintended and unwelcome education one gets in times of war. It certainly is not normal for a little child to have knowledge of parachutes, bombs, or missiles. (Although I realize that is quite common in the Middle East today—unfortunately!)

Mama often talked about the falling bombs. "First" she said, "They looked like cigars, as they fell from the airplanes, but grew to look bigger and bigger as they neared their targets." Again, this was in the countryside where an airstrike could sometimes be observed from a safe distance.

At this evacuation, Fritz was with us. We were split up: my mother and I at one farmer and Manfred and Fritz at another. Fritz, who is now a gospel minister, definitely had an early calling from God. According to Mama, Fritz was quietly reading the Bible at this young age. He was also an honest boy. My brothers liked to roam in the woods around the farmland. On one of those outdoor explorations, they found a bottle of wine. It was not unusual to find something left behind by a military unit traveling through the area.

Fritz gave the bottle to the host farmer. Mama praised him for being honest, but also told him the bottle of wine could have come in handy as a bartering item. When the food supply was low and money was running out, people used to barter whatever they had to make ends meet.

Another thing I remember during this evacuation is that Mama gave me my first religious instruction. She had taught me little bedtime prayers, but this was different. It happened the night "Santa Claus" came to visit.

On this particular night, we were all gathered in a semicircle around the fireplace in the parlor. It did not happen too often that we sat with the farmer's family, but this night was special. I can see the room in my mind's eye. The floor had black and white ceramic tiles with a beautiful area rug. The entrance consisted of a French door with a small foyer behind it and the door to the outside. Across from the door was the fireplace with black marble all around.

I watched the flames while the grown-ups talked about the war. Then the doorbell rang. The farmer got up and opened the door and brought in "Santa Claus." I never saw anybody dressed like that. He was wearing a big red shirt, a red hat and had a white beard and mustache. This was totally strange to me. With the war going on for about five years at that point, I don't remember any Christmas celebration, any Christmas decoration, or any special holiday for that matter.

"Santa" approached us, looking intently at all the children, then asking in a deep voice, "Have you all been good children this year?" I had no idea what was going on, but the farmer's children assured Santa that they were very good indeed. After that Santa handed out presents. Now my interest was aroused. *Would I get a present?*

My heart beat a little faster when he stopped in front of me. Whoa! He handed me a gift, wrapped in colorful paper.

The room was filled with excitement. All the kids were opening their gifts. I looked at Mama.

She said, "Go ahead—open it."

Well, she did not have to say that again. I removed the paper and found a little box inside. It was just a what-not box, but what amazed me was the decoration on it. The background was a brown-black varnish with straw cut in different shapes and glued on top and the sides to make an exquisite design. I just loved it.

I found out later that the box was made by Russian soldiers. The farmer found the soldiers in the woods. Since the men were wounded, the farmers had compassion on them and took them home. Isn't it amazing how ordinary people always help each other, even if the person in need is from the enemy camp?

Back to my religious instruction. When we were back in our room after the celebration, Mama put me on the top bunk bed. "Helga, I want you to know, there is no such person as Santa Claus. We celebrate Christmas, because God sent his Son into the world to save us from sin and take us into heaven after we die. The person you have seen tonight was the farmer's oldest son, dressed up as Santa Claus. This is a Catholic tradition to remember St. Nickolas. Legend has it that he was a good monk who helped people in need. Now the Catholic people honor him by giving gifts and spreading goodwill."

I had no idea who or what Catholic people were, nor did I have any idea what kind of people we were. Yet the incident stuck in my mind.

It is very common that if kids have an experience that touched them deeply, they share it with other kids—right? Who could blame me for telling my playmate, the farmer's youngest daughter, "You know, there is really no such person as 'Santa Claus.' That was your brother last night." Ouch!

She immediately ran to her mother and wanted to know if I was telling the truth. Poor Mama had to stand and listen to a lecture from the man of the house that it was his business to tell his children whether Santa Claus is real or not.

I don't remember if I got a scolding from my mother. If I did, that did not stand out as much as "meeting Santa Claus."

Young Anna Lenk (Schweichel)

Traute an Elsbeth   Frieda and Elsbeth

Manfred and Fritz in front of the Lenk's house

Manfred and Fritz

Helga, two years old   Helga, fifteen years old

Manfred, eleven years old

Family in front of house, except Traute

Mother and Father in front of house entrance

Papa as a miner   Helga and Papa making music

Guenther and Elsbeth

Frieda and Helmet   Christa, Manfred and Brian

Helga in front of bunker (2004)

Fritz and his sisters
Frieda, Traute, Elsbeth, Helga, L-R

Tatzmanns leaving Germany

Chapter 11
An Episode from Frieda's Life as Recorded in Her Journal

Frieda

By the time I was old enough to go to *Pflichtjahr*, I had already been away from home three times. This was because many children my age were undernourished. The government took action and sent the effected children to *Erholungsheime* (recovery homes) where children received better food—even if it was just for a brief period of time. I was a skinny child, but had thick braids. My mother often said, "all the nourishment seems to go into your hair."

I was only fourteen years old and was sad that I had to leave home again. But we had to obey the laws. I was assigned to a farmer in Muenster. The situation in that home was a rather peculiar one.

The owner of the home was serving in the Wehrmacht, but the lady of the house took her sick brother in. He really could not do any work, but there is a lot of work to be done on a farm. When my employer heard about a soldier who had deserted the Polish army, she took him in and hid him from the authorities. He was so thankful for her kindness that in return he did all the jobs men do around a farm.

I had to do the housework but also helped with the care of the animals. I learned how to milk a cow and feed the pigs and the chickens. Besides all that, I helped with the gardening and did the laundry. The water supply came from a pump on the land. To work the pump was very hard for me, because my arms lacked the muscles necessary to activate it.

After I was there for some time, the brother of my employer died. The family were practicing Catholics. Of course, I had to attend the funeral, and that's how I experienced a Catholic Mass. The Mass was totally different from what I knew of church services. Personally, I practiced what my parents taught me at home. Papa would read a passage from the Bible, and we would kneel down at the kitchen chairs to pray. I had my Bible with me at the farm and kept up with that tradition.

I liked the Muenster area, because it was out in the country and consisted mainly of farmland. There were no enemy attacks and we had plenty of food.

Soon my *Pflichtjahr* was over and I had to go home. There, I had to start my career. I wanted to be a kindergarten teacher. This required that I work in a household with several children. This was called *Anerkannte Lehrstelle* (literally recognized apprenticeship—like an internship). The family had four children—two boys and two girls—spanning in age from newborn to seven years of age. I loved the kids and they loved me.

My mother came with me to sign the apprenticeship contract. The family lived close to the Holland border, not far from where my mother and my three younger siblings were later evacuated.

The apprenticeship required that I attend trade school once a week. For this I had to take the train to Gronau, a city in Holland. I enjoyed the train ride and going to the city. Unfortunately, this did not last long. The war disrupted life everywhere.

Allied planes were attacking the trains and the cities. My employer had a brother in Paderborn where the fighting was felt less. He invited his sister to stay with him for a while. When we got there, he said I was not invited, but then let me stay anyway. I worked in the kitchen and the garden and helped with the children. After some weeks we went back to Muenster.

These were the last two years of the war. The husband of the lady I worked for was still serving in the armed forces. Unfortunately, when the war was already in the last phase, she received a letter that her husband was killed in action. She was only thirty-six years old. It was heartbreaking. I felt sorry and unable to console her. She was so young and now she had to raise those children all by herself. How tragic!

More and more people believed that Germany was losing the war. British and Scottish troops marched into Holland and Northern Germany. People were scared to death and were at a loss about what to do.

When my employer heard that some neighbors went into the woods to hide, she decided to do the same. We put up tents for shelter from the environment. We could hear a lot of gunfire in the distance, but did not see anybody. This lasted for about four or five days.

Then the noise was replaced by an eerie stillness. Everybody wondered what was going on.

In the meantime, foreign soldiers were searching in the woods for civilians. When they finally found us, they assured us that we didn't have to be afraid. They had no intention to harm us. But the best news they brought was that the war was over!

We could hardly believe it. It took a while to comprehend the news, but finally we all breathed a sigh of relief. Everybody was happy. Six long years of misery had finally come to an end.

My mother, with Manfred and Helga, went home right away from their place of evacuation. Fritz stayed a little longer with the farmer. He was useful to them to help with the farm work. Especially because it took some time for the surviving soldiers to return home.

I stayed with my employer family until 1946, because I had to finish my apprenticeship.

The good news that the war was over did not brighten my employer. Her husband would not come home.

Traute and Herbert's Wedding Day 1945

Chapter 12
The Conclusion of Traute's Love Story

Traute

In my earlier years, I attended cooking classes given by the mine company. Now I was employed as a cook at a boys group home. The building was a hotel, but had been converted to accommodate one of the youth camps Hitler set up for boys between the ages of fourteen and eighteen. When the war ended, I was still employed at the hotel turned boy's home in the Northeastern part of Germany. Not too far from the hotel was an army post. This post was receiving soldiers coming back from the Eastern Front. Before the soldiers could go home, they had to be counted and registered. One might say it was fate that Herbert was among those soldiers.

Through the grapevine, Herbert heard that I was working at the boy's home. He got all excited and had to find out if it was true. As soon as he had the opportunity, he went to his superior officer and asked for permission to visit me.

I could not believe my eyes when I saw Herbert in the lobby. How could this be? I thought he was in France.

My questions could wait—first I ran into his arms. Our tears mingled on our cheeks as we embraced each other.

In our conversation, I found out that after France, Herbert was sent to the Russian Front. I was so happy he was alive.

When the other soldiers found out there was an engaged couple among them, they all persuaded us to get married. Everybody thought it would be wonderful to have a happy celebration after all the misery we had been through.

This was not how I envisioned my wedding. I had daydreams of marrying in a white gown, but I did not see any possibility of doing that. How could I? Such items were not available where I was—or were they?

It so happened that an actress was staying at the hotel to entertain the troops. She generously offered me one of her white evening gowns to wear. Now my heart was filled with joy and anticipation.

As for Herbert, he could still wear one of his better uniforms; it would be a suitable substitute for a tuxedo.

So it was settled. We would get married.

Elsbeth

I could hardly believe that Herbert happened to come to the same area where Traute was working and where I had joined her after I lost my job. I guess they were meant for each other—no matter what my parents felt. Postal service had not been established yet. All communications were broken down. We could not even notify our parents. So I was the only one from the family at the wedding.

Could they have waited? Of course. However, there was more involved than being reunited in love. Being married to Traute, Herbert could use her address as his home address. As an Austrian soldier, he would have been sent to France as a prisoner of war until the Allies created order out of chaos. So Traute and Herbert were married in front of a justice of the peace on June 24, 1945.

When Herbert's time came to be discharged, all three of us went home. We were a little apprehensive, not knowing what we would find. Everywhere we looked, things were in ruins. Would our house still be there? Did Papa survive?

Yes, thank God, our house did not get damaged in all those air raids. Papa survived and was still working in the coal mine.

The next question was: where would we find space for everybody in four rooms? Our grandma was also still living with us. Papa used his creative side. My parents gave up their bedroom for the newlyweds and slept on the pull-out sofa in the living room. He added a bed for me in grandma's room. After that Papa built another bedroom in the attic for Manfred and Helga. Frieda and Fritz were not home yet, so for a while the arrangement worked fine. We also knew it would be only a matter of time until Herbert received permission to return to Austria.

Of course, Traute would accompany him and that made all of us a little sad.

PART TWO

Reconnection of Families and Restoration of Country

Chapter 13
The War Is Over

Helga

Finally, after six long years, the war ended on May 18, 1945. Germany was divided by the Allied countries: England, France, Russia, and the United States of America. We lived in the part that was occupied by the Americans.

With the help of the Allies, life began returning to normal. Of course, this I say as an adult. How could I have known what it means to live a normal life? All I had experienced so far was war—running to shelters, being evacuated, hearing sirens, and seeing a lot of houses destroyed.

Part of the "normal" life was the reinstating of the postal service. Among the first mail we received was a postcard from Traute and Herbert. It brought us the big news that Herbert had returned from the front to the same area where Traute worked and that they got married! Well, what do you know? Love prevailed after all!

The local administrations also worked hard to normalize the school systems. I was about to enter first grade when another disaster hit out town.

The Flood

We heard someone yelling in the street, "The Emscher Dam broke! The Emscher Dam broke!"

"What are you yelling about?" People asked stupefied, rising from their evening meals.

"Hurry, get your stuff up to the second floor," answered those who had already seen the water approaching in the distance.

There was instant chaos. Papa and Mama sprang into action. They tried to make decisions fast. What do we need? What do we have to save? How high would the water go? Can we even stay here? Papa dispatched orders like a general.

Elsbeth, Manfred, and I formed an assembly line on the stairway as our parents handed us whatever they wanted to save.

The water came fast. Soon it was in our street. Then it climbed the five stone steps leading to the foyer. When it entered the first floor, Papa told Mother to stay on the stairs too. Soon the water level was up to Papa's waist and kept flowing in.

Our wooden chairs began to float. Mother was worried that the china cabinet would topple and fall on Papa. She urged him to come up. Throughout all of the commotion, Grandma was sending prayers heavenwards. Papa only managed short pleadings: "Help us, Lord!"

God answered their prayers—the water leveled off at the second-to-last step.

I do not know how I slept the first night. As a kid, I probably slept right through. But I can imagine that my parents kept watching the water to make sure it really stopped.

The next day the American soldiers came with a rowboat to check on us. They brought us drinking water and said they would return to bring Grandmother to one of her other daughters so we would have more room.

When the water did not recede after a few days, people started to be creative. Some tried to build crude rafts, others swam to the elevated train trestle behind their gardens. Papa built his own version of a boat. Since tools and other things were needed to do anything, Papa was really resourceful.

Our foyer was attached like a porch to the side of the house. The roof of it reached just under Grandma's window. Papa and Manfred climbed on top of it and from there managed to reach the washhouse. I don't know how they were able to get what they needed, but they came back with our galvanized bathtub and two empty propane bottles. The bathtub was at least five feet long. Papa attached the propane containers with some wooden boards on the side of bathtub, and so created a boat strong enough to carry Manfred and one other person.

People who had built themselves rafts pulled themselves along the streetcar cables—which had no electricity in them at the time. It is amazing what people can do with the little material available to them.

Manfred was able to help some neighbors get to the train trestle. The water was only in the southern part of the town. Once people reached the railroad tracks, they could walk to where the water leveled off.

The Americans arranged for the children to have one warm meal a day in a restaurant. That was fun! Manfred and I walked along the railroad tracks to a tavern about a kilometer away and enjoyed a warm meal.

Then there was also a comical situation.

Elsbeth was an attractive eighteen-year-old, which did not go unnoticed by the neighborhood boys. One boy lived in an apartment complex behind our garden. When he saw Papa's "boat," he thought to himself *this is a clever way to visit Elsbeth.*

He lowered his tub into the water and then lowered himself into it—only to sink right into the water with the tub! He didn't know that Papa had reinforced the tub to make it float.

Luckily, the boy could swim.

Mother, who had watched the whole episode, got a good laugh out of it.

I forgot to mention one big item—the Emscher River was an open sewer. I can't imagine what it must have felt like to swim in sewer water!

There were coal mines underneath this part of town, which was, lower than the northern part. Telltale cracks were seen on most buildings. They were also smoke covered from all the coal dust. My brother-in-law, who lived in Essen, said one could see the smog when the streetcar approached a certain section on the way.

Meanwhile, my sister Frieda had finished her apprenticeship and was on her way home. She traveled by streetcar, which stopped at the town hall, from which she would take another streetcar to the southern part of the town.

It was late at night, and Frieda did not see the connecting streetcar. She thought service had already stopped because of the late hour. So she started walking toward our house.

Then she realized that nobody was walking in her direction. Soon she saw something strange in the distance. *What is that?* she wondered. *It looks like water is covering the street.* When she got closer—sure enough—it was water. She wondered, *What happened? Where did the water come from?*

Luckily for her, our Aunt Liese lived close by.

So she walked, always keeping one eye on the water, until she reached my aunt's apartment.

Aunt Liese filled her in about the break of the Emscher Dam. Then she made a bed for Frieda on the sofa and told her to spend the night.

The next morning, Frieda walked along the railroad tracks until she was across from our house. There she yelled as loud as she could to get someone's attention.

Finally, one of our neighbors heard her and yelled to the next neighbor, who yelled over to our house.

Manfred was happy to be of service with his water taxi to go out there and bring his sister home.

The flood lasted for about six weeks. The water receded slowly, centimeter by centimeter and meter by meter. Most items that were in the water were badly damaged or even ruined. The wallpaper peeled off the walls and everything else needed to be scrubbed down and given a fresh coat of paint.

After some time, the governing authorities rewarded all flood victims with household items or money—sometimes both.

I remember how exited Mama got when we received a new set of dishes. The name brand on them was Rosenthal, known even today for their fine china. Mother treasured it very much. She even brought it to the United States when she immigrated in 1960.

Over the years more and more pieces were broken, but my sister kept a few pieces, just for memory's sake.

Essen during WWII

Chapter 14
Elsbeth's Career

Helga

Once the war was over, people tried to have a normal life. Families that had been scattered looked for each other to reconnect. Refugees tried to find housing and unemployed people tried to find jobs.

Elsbeth

Since my apprenticeship at Krupp was interrupted by the bombing, I never finished my education. Now that the war was over, I had to look for a job. Life had not returned to normal in Germany yet. The Allies still occupied the country. I could not pick and choose what I wanted to do, because employers were still in the process of rebuilding what was damaged during the war.

The procedure was to go to the unemployment office and take any job that was available and that the officers decided one was capable of. I was offered a job in a factory in Bielefeld, some distance from my hometown. All workers were given room and board, because most girls came from other cities.

We lived in army barracks which were now empty. One section of it was separated from our barracks and was used to house delinquent girls who had been taken out of their homes. A nurse was living with them to watch over them.

The factory produced yarn made from flax. The flax was on spindles which had to be in water. For reasons unknown to me, this created a terrible odor. Most of the other girls did not seem to mind, but I could not stand the smell. It was so bad that I asked for another job.

The management took pity on me and let me work in the kitchen.

The cook was a highly-educated woman in her late forties. However, since she had previously worked in Hitler's government, she was here to be intellectually reprogrammed. Evidently she was capable of a white collar job, but had to do this hands-on job in the kitchen. Our supervisor watched over her—how she behaved and how her conversations went with her co-workers.

All that was not a concern of mine and we became good friends. I actually learned a great deal from her.

Working in the kitchen, I also had the opportunity to meet other people. One of them was another nurse whose job it was to check on the delinquent girls. After she finished her inspection, she liked to linger in the kitchen for a while. She shared many things about nursing. The more she told me about her job, the more interested I became until I finally made up my mind to pursue a career in nursing.

I send a resume to the Lutheran Mother House, which functioned as a placement center for girls who wanted to be nurses. To my great joy, I was accepted. For an apprenticeship, I had to sign a contract for three years.

My first placement station was in Hamburg. I worked in a hospital and also went to school for the theoretical part of the training. I really liked it there. The bad part is that Germany had just gone through six years of war. There were shortages on almost everything that makes a hospital function smoothly: medications, instruments, even doctors. It is my opinion that lives could have been saved under better circumstances. I was too young to offer an opinion about the running of the hospital, but it does not take rocket science to see the truth of this.

My second station was in the city of Dahmen in Mecklenburg. This was the same city I was in with Traute the last part of the war.

In 1948, I received a letter from my father that changed my life drastically. He informed me that my mother had a change-of-life pregnancy. Mother was forty-seven years old. Maybe that was too old for her to have a baby. She miscarried. Papa wrote further that Mother was unwell.

I asked for a week of vacation to go home. I helped with the household chores and gave Mother some rest. Thank God, she recovered. However, things changed for me. Being with family and going to church with them, I realized how much I missed that. I believe the sorrow felt throughout the war made everyone a little numb. All the separations from family and friends during the last six years worked on people's emotional well-being. During the war, one only thought about coping with hunger, surviving airstrikes, and staying safe. Emotions were pushed deep down inside.

Now that the danger of falling bombs and burning houses had ended, the emotions I had suppressed came to the surface again. I re-evaluated my life. I longed to be home again. It seemed like nothing else mattered.

I decided to go back and ask my employer to let me out of the contract. That was not an easy task. I prayed about it and asked God to give me wisdom.

There was a certain procedure one had to follow to get out of an apprenticeship. I had to get several signatures from my co-workers who agreed with me that it would be better for my emotional health to return to my family. Now, the correct way was to ask the head nurse first and after that ask other people who agreed with me. However, I went to the other people first and then to the head nurse.

She looked at me with a strange expression on her face. "After you got all the other signatures, what can I do?" She signed the papers for me to get out of the contract.

I praised God for answering my prayer. I felt happy and free.

Chapter 15
Treasure Hunting in the Ruins

Helga

Our house did not get damaged during all the air raids over our town, but there were ruins all around us. The German population suffered great material losses. People rummaged in the ruins to see what could be salvaged. Handymen looked for building material that could be reused. A person walking in my neighborhood, on any given day, would observe all kinds of people working in the ruins.

Almost everybody was involved in cleaning bricks. The old mortar had to be carefully chipped away so the bricks did not get damaged in the process and could be used again. Even I, as little as I was, maybe seven or eight years old, became skillful in hammering at the mortar and keeping the brick intact.

Manfred and I worked together. This assured my parents that I did not get hurt working with a hammer and a chisel. Whenever we had a certain amount of bricks cleaned, we sold them to anybody who was willing to pay for them. There was never any shortage of people buying bricks. In a way, this helped with the cleanup and the restoration of the cities. Most houses around our neighborhood were not privately owned, but belonged to the coal mine corporation. They did not object to our activity.

Speaking of coal mines, I remember there was also a lot of coal left in the cellars. This was a precious commodity, because it was the major fuel for heating. Since my father was a coal miner, we received our coal free of charge. Other people had to purchase the coal.

I had a classmate named Frieda, who lived across from our house. Her father had a problem with alcohol. He could not keep a job for very long and so the family was suffering financially. Frieda wanted to help the family and came up with the idea to extract the coal out of the basements of the ruins. She recruited me for this dreadful job. Dreadful, because coal is very dirty. Another idea of hers was to collect bottles and sell them to the local tavern. Poverty sometimes creates streetwise kids.

My brother Manfred and his friends also had ideas on how to make money. A Lutheran church in the neighborhood was severely damaged. Manfred and his two friends thought the copper on the steeple clock would be worth some money. So, they devised a plan to get the clock down. Unfortunately, they were caught red-handed.

This resulted in a visit from the pastor of the church. My parents were shocked when they heard why the pastor had come to their house.

Manfred received his rightful punishment. Yes, my father believed in corporal punishment and I think it was an effective way to raise children—if it was handled correctly! Papa explained that his actions were based on biblical teaching (Proverbs 13:24).

Relief From an Unexpected Source

It took some time after the war ended for the infrastructure to be fully in place. Scarcity of life's basic necessaries made life miserable. If people had anything of value, they would barter it for food or whatever they needed.

The lines at the local bakery were always long. One had to go early in the morning, before the bread was sold out for the day. Poverty was all around us.

Then something wonderful happened. We began to receive CARE (Cooperative for American Relief Everywhere, Inc.) packages, filled with clothing and food items. The CARE packages were mainly distributed through local churches. Not surprisingly, our church membership increased tremendously.

After all this time, I can think of specific items from those packages in detail.

Among the food items we received canned plum pudding, Saltine crackers and cornmeal. From the clothing, I recollect a plaid skirt and a wonderful tweed jacket. But nothing pleased me more than a faux fur coat!

I wore clothing from those donation for three or four years after the war. I am very grateful for the CARE Relief organization for what they did and are still doing today.

Chapter 16
Entering School

Helga

I was lucky to be at the right age to enter school in 1945. I say lucky because Fritz and Manfred missed a lot of school during the war. At least I was able to start with first grade and keep on going without any interruptions.

It was still a custom at the time to start school with a blackboard and chalk. I keep repeating myself about the devastations of the war, but how else can I describe the circumstances that we had to cope with? The stores had very little to offer in terms of school supplies. So my father searched for the smoothest slate roof tile he could find, sanded it down a bit, and that was my blackboard.

I was a little embarrassed to go to school with a roof tile for a blackboard, but what could I do? After a few days, a welcome surprise came my way. My teacher was very familiar with the Lenk family, because she had already taught my older siblings. I have no idea how old she was, since my oldest sister is fourteen years older than I, but again, there was also a shortage of teachers. Male teachers may have died serving the country or might still have been in prisoner of war camps. In any case, my teacher took pity on me and presented me with a nice blackboard with a proper wooden frame around it. She asked me to come forward and give her a kiss. Another embarrassment, but this time I took it in good stride, kissed her on the cheek, and took the blackboard.

Many young children suffered from malnutrition after the war. For this reason, the Americans provided school lunches. My favorite was hot Cream of Farina with raisins. To supplement the protein in our diet, we were given cod liver oil. At the time it did not come in easy-to-swallow capsules; it came in liquid form in a big bottle. That meant we had to stand in line and be spoon-fed by a nurse. We had to open our mouths and swallow the horrible-tasting liquid. Of course, I realize today that it was very good for us.

Erholung — Recovery

Besides the school lunches, some children were send to *Erholungsheime* (health recovery homes). These were mainly located in the countryside, away from the polluted cities. I was send to a mountainous region, the famous Teutoburger Wald (Teutoburg Forest). The mountain's fame came from the fact that there, in AD 9, the Germanic tribes were victorious over the Roman army.

This was the first time I was sent away from home. It must have been in the fall, because I remember walking through beautiful fall-colored woods. The ground was covered with thick leaves, which we kicked as we were walking. This was a nice contrast to brick buildings, cement sidewalks, and asphalt streets back home. I noticed the air smelled fresh, not polluted as I was used to. The time spent in the homes lasted about three weeks. We played indoor and outdoor games, helped in the kitchen, and listened to stories told by one of the workers. I was a little homesick, but all in all, I enjoyed being there.

Back to My School Years

I do not know if the German school system is still set up the way it was when I went to school, but this is how it was in my time: Up to the fourth grade all students were together. In fourth grade, we were given a test to determine who qualified for higher education. The high achievers were encouraged to enter the higher education route—first to the gymnasium, then high school, and the university if that was their desire.

The rest would stay in elementary school until eighth grade. After that they would chose a trade. One would enter into an apprenticeship for three years and go to a trade school once a week. This was the system my sisters went through.

I stayed in grade school. However, special opportunities were given even there. For example, one could learn a second language, which was voluntary at the time. When English was offered, I signed up. The class took place at seven o'clock, one hour before regular school started.

After six months, I could not endure the teacher's temper anymore. He yelled and threw chalk and other small items at us. There were rumors that he suffered a head wound during the war and his brain was impaired.

I told my mother, "I can't take it anymore. The teacher is mean."

I am glad Mother understood and let me drop the class. Shortly thereafter, the teacher was fired. Evidently, the school administration realized he was not fit to teach.

In seventh grade, shorthand was offered for students who wanted to find secretarial employment. I signed up again. Students had to pay a fee for extracurricular classes. Mama was generous enough to give me the money.

Unfortunately, two months into my studies, she got sick and had to be hospitalized. I had no choice but to drop the class again.

Papa did not think I needed shorthand and therefore did not give me the money. He said I also had to help with the household chores more since Mama was sick.

I had one more chance to take English as a second language. It was in eighth grade. Slowly, the school added more teachers as times improved. Now the language courses were taught from fifth grade on. Since I was in eighth grade,

English was not on my schedule, but I could go during one of the other classes.

It so happened that English was offered during our math class. I made a pact with my girlfriend Edith that I would write some composition papers for her in return for her teaching me math.

Somehow, we both graduated with decent grades. I am not disclosing what our grades were, but I can tell you that my grade in English was higher than in math. That's where my interest was.

Chapter 17
Death in the Ruins

Helga

Children were not allowed to play in the ruins because of hanging beams and loose bricks. Accidents could happen if one was not careful. However, as the old saying goes "boys will be boys," and that was certainly true of Manfred and his two friends, Willy and Walter.

One sunny afternoon they were playing in the ruins of a former hardware store. The storefront window was blown out and half the floor was missing—leaving a gaping hole to the basement. Snooping around for anything interesting, they found a strange-looking metal container. Their curiosity was aroused. They had to find out what was inside, but there was nothing that looked like an opening. How could they open it? One of the boys had the outrageous idea of standing on the windowsill and throwing the unknown object onto the broken floor and see if they could open "this thing."

To be fair in their task, they decided that each got to throw this object six times. Just then my mother called Manfred to come home. She needed a loaf of bread and she wanted to send him to the grocery store. Manfred obeyed Mama and got the bread. I was just walking by as he came out of the store.

"Oh, Helga, do me a favor and bring the bread home for me." He handed me the bag. The moment I entered our house, a horrible noise shattered the air. Mama saw me with the bread and screamed, "Where is Manfred?'

She did not even wait for an answer, but ran out of the house to see what happened. Smoke filled the air and flames leaped from the old hardware store. There was instant chaos. Manfred was nowhere in sight.

Later we heard that Willy had been holding the object over his head as Manfred came back on the scene. It was his seventh throw!

"It's my turn," Manfred said.

However, since Willy's hands were already high over his head, he finished his throw and hurled the object onto the concrete floors-slab.

This resulted in an explosion. What the boys thought to be a gasoline tank was a bomb!

Willy was so dumbfounded he lost his balance and fell into the store.

My mother found Willy's mother holding her boy after he was rescued from the flames. His ten-year-old body had shrunk to the size of a four-year-old. It was heartbreaking!

Sadly, even though he was rushed to the hospital, there was really nothing that could be done for him. He had to endure the excruciating pain for another six hours before death put an end to it.

I have no idea if painkillers were available at that time. The year was 1947, just two years after the war. It is just so hard to think about it that one wishes his suffering could have been somewhat lessened.

Someone pushed Walter into a water puddle to extinguish his burning clothing. Mama was frantic! Since she could not find Manfred on the scene, she came back home. There was Manfred leaning over the sink, sobbing, as he tried to cool his open wounds with running cold water. The most tragic thing was that the average household had no telephone. If ambulances existed at the time, I never saw or heard one.

In desperation, Mama called Fritz to help her carry Manfred to our family doctor as fast as possible. The doctor's office was about five blocks away from our house.

It turned out that they had found a phosphorus bomb, which is highly flammable and spreads fast. Parts of the bomb flew all the way across to the other side of the street.

The doctor tried to explain to my mother, "A phosphorescent substance on the skin keeps spreading. The only way to stop it is to 'burn' it out with another chemical."

I cannot imagine the pain Manfred must have endured. The doctor ordered the wounds to be kept open during the daytime—without bandages. He assured my mother that this would speed up the healing process.

When my father came home from work, he was horrified by how Manfred looked. He said, "I should give you a spanking for playing in the ruins, but where would I hit? Besides, the pain you must feel is plenty of punishment."

Manfred had wounds all over. We counted thirty-six on his body alone. On one side of his face he had small wounds one next to the other. They were about the size of a child's pinky fingernail. Manfred could not walk around too much. He was confined to the bed or a lounge chair, always reclining on a clean sheet, clad only in shorts. Whenever the weather was warm enough to sit outside, we would put the chair in our garden behind the house. The sunshine felt good on his wounds, but would turn to pain later on. Often I would entertain him by singing Sunday school songs to him. A particular one he liked to hear was, *"Gott ist die Liebe, lässt mich erlösen . . ."* (God is love, he will save me).

A theological question: Can God bring comfort to someone through an eight-year-old girl singing songs? I may be conceited, but I think He can!

Will it surprise you that we played "war games?" It should not.

The previous incident was tragic, but the war was still fresh in our minds. The fact is that children like to act out things that affect them deeply.

There are two games I remember.

One was drawing a large circle on the ground, dividing it up with lines like a pie. In each slice, we drew the name of a country—France, England, America, Russia, depending on how many kids participated in the game. Then one would call out, "I declare war on _____," and would ran away as fast as possible as he was pursued by the "enemy." The captured one would then be out of the game and the victorious one would get another slice of the "pie" and so on until somebody owned the entire circle.

In another game the boys liked to play, they formed two rows facing each other and bombarded the opponent with small pebbles. Most of the time the kids from the entire neighborhood played together, but on this game the girls liked to be spectators rather than participants. Okay, the stones were supposed to be small enough that they would not seriously hurt anybody. However, as I said before, "boys will be boys," and their foolishness resulted in two incidents. One was that a bigger rock hit my one-and-only doll and smashed its porcelain head. It made me cry, because I treasured that doll. It was a hand-me-down from my sister Frieda.

I cuddled my doll, crying as I showed it to my mother.

My parents had no extra money to purchase another doll. Stores did not have all merchandise available either. But Mother remembered when Christmastime came. My gift that year was a brand-new doll! I took very good care of it.

The second incident was that a rock from the opposing team hit Manfred on the head. I don't remember if that was before or after the bomb explosion. In any case, the rock hit him with enough force that blood trickled down his face, but it was not serious. His friends took a ladder and put Manfred on top of it. Then four boys, each grabbing a corner, carried him home singing, *"Ich hat einen Kameraden ..."*

It is such a touching song that I will give a paraphrased translation:

> Once I had a comrade
> A better one you will not find.
> We walked together
> side by side;
> Our steps in unison.
> A bullet came flying
> was it meant for you or me?
> It tore him down
> he is lying at my feet—
> As if he were a part of me.
> He reaches up to touch my hand

while he is lying there;
His hands can't reach me anymore …
Stay in the eternal life—my best comrade."

Manfred was not seriously injured, as I already mentioned, so the song was part of the play-acting.

Many of the songs we sang at the time were melancholic, describing medieval heroic deeds, unfulfilled or forbidden love stories, and so on. I loved those songs. They were often sung around the campfire.

We still sing them occasionally when we visit our relatives in Germany and do any traveling by car.

My First Memorable Postwar Christmas

The war ended in May 1945. The following two Christmases don't stand out in my mind. The one that stands out is Christmas 1947.

Some days before Christmas, I helped my mother bake Christmas cookies. Mother had a good cookie press. It could be attached to the table, with the handle hanging free on the side. My favorite cookies were *Spritzgebäck* (butter shortbread). My mother fed the dough into the cookie machine, and turned the handle while I cut off the pieces and laid them on a cookie sheet. After they were baked, we brushed melted chocolate or lemon and sugar on one half of the cookies. I also remember taking the peels off the almonds for the *Spekulatius* cookies. This activity and the wonderful smell of baking cookies filled me with anticipation of things to come.

Christmas was celebrated with a real live tree on December 24. In our family, the children had to wait in the kitchen or outside while the parents set up the tree and put the presents underneath. When everything was ready, my parents sang, *"Ihr Kinderlein kommet, oh kommet doch all ...* (children come, come all). They did not have to repeat the invitation; we were ready!

On Christmas in 1947, I received my first doll. I also received a stuffed animal that Elsbeth made for me. Manfred received, among other things, a domino set. We enjoyed many hours playing with it.

The goodies were portioned out for each person. Mother filled a colorful aluminum plate with cookies, nuts, candies, and chocolate. Manfred and I even made a game out of that. We set up a cup and from a short distance and threw nuts into it, competing to see who would be first to fill the cup.

Later, Papa played the zither and we sang many, many Christmas carols. The tree was decorated with real candles. We had a special clip-on device that had a place in the middle for the candle and a "skirt" underneath to catch the wax. The candles were lit only on Christmas Eve. When we were done playing and singing, the flames were extinguished and it was time for bed.

Stille Nacht, Heilige Nacht / Alles schläft einsam wacht ...

Evangelical believers did not display a crèche. I assume it has something to do with not having "graven images," similar to why they don't have crosses with a figure of Jesus on them. The emphasis was on God sending his Son into the world.

We also celebrated at the church school. I don't remember which day, but I remember it was at nights. We sang a lot of carols and had a short message. However, the children received a bag with cookies, an apple, and nuts. I remember walking home on the cold winter nights, nibbling on cookies and looking at the stars. After all, we just heard how the angels proclaimed the glorious message to the shepherds. It all added to the celebratory atmosphere.

My father made me a muffler from rabbit fur. That was a wonderful thing to keep my hands warm. We had our own rabbits. It was a very common meat supply at the time.

Christmas is a wonderful time of the year.

Chapter 18
A New Government

Helga

About three years after the war, the Allies were ready to negotiate with the Germans to establish a new government. This called for a general democratic election.

Suddenly, political slogans appeared everywhere. Europe has many kiosks. They are round columns about three or four feet in diameter and about ten feet high. These kiosks are for advertising anything, including movies, concerts, lost animals, and current events.

During Hitler's time, they were covered with political themes. I remember one that featured a man with a black trench coat with his finger over his mouth. The words underneath read: *Psst, der Feind hört mit!* (Psst, the enemy is listening).

Now the new political parties put up their flyers. Manfred and I had not experienced what it was like in the early thirties when Hitler came to power. Manfred was born 1936, and I was born 1939. But even as children we were drawn into all the excitement of the adult world. We made our own flyers, showing which party we favored and hanging them all over the kitchen. The parties we chose were not out of personal conviction, rather they were a reflection of what we saw all around us.

One of the most verbal candidates was Konrad Adenauer. According to a BBC History report, he "set about forming a new political party, the Christian Democratic Union (CDU). In 1948, he was made president of the parliamentary council which drew up a constitution for the three western zones of Germany." He was elected chancellor of the Federal Republic of Germany on September 15, 1949.

Another important piece of information from the BBC report:

> Adenauer was particularly keen to encourage closer ties with the USA and France. He opened

diplomatic relations with the USSR and Eastern European communist nations, but refused to recognize the German Democratic Republic (East Germany). Adenauer also negotiated a compensation agreement with Israel in recognition of the crimes perpetrated against the Jews by Nazis.[2]

Missing in Action? Prisoners of War? Where are our loved ones?

In the years immediately following the end of the war, soldiers returned home from the various fronts or prisoner of war camps. Earlier in my story, I mentioned my uncle Herman. My grandmother, who was living with us, still hoped he was alive. My aunt had not received anything about his whereabouts. No missing in action or death notice.

So Grandmother was anxiously awaiting some kind of news. The last Aunt Lieise heard was that he was sent to the Russian front. Grandma and my aunt sent letters with a picture to the Red Cross, who did an excellent job of reconnecting people all over Europe. Local towns and cities put up bulletin boards in their town halls and especially at train stations. People hoped that someone coming home

---

[2] "Konrad Adenauer (1876-1967)," BBC,
http://www.bbc.co.uk/history/historic_figures/adenauer_konrad.shtml

from the front would recognize the person in the picture and bring (hopefully) good news to the seeking family.

Days turned into weeks and week turned into years— my uncle did not come home. Aunt Liese never remarried. She raised her three children all by herself.

However, two soldiers of interest to my story had returned from the fronts—one from France and one from the United States of America. They became my brothers-in-law.

Chapter 19
Romance Enters the Lives of Two Sisters

Elsbeth

When I received the letter from my father about mother's illness, I did what was necessary to quit my apprenticeship and got my wish to return home.

The first day I was home, Frieda informed me that there would be a Sunday school meeting in our home. "Guenther will also come."

If there was a hidden meaning in her words, I missed it. Frieda and Fritz taught Sunday school and Guenther, who played the violin and loved music, helped with the songs. There was no Sunday school curriculum available, but Papa knew the Bible well and helped Fritz and Frieda prepare the lessons.

Guenther had been a prisoner of war in an American camp in France. He was discharged in the fall of 1946. I had never met him before. When I came down the stairs from our second story, there he was sitting in the living room with the others. I believe I stared at him. I wonder if I blushed? He had wavy blond hair and deep blue eyes. Our eyes met, and I fell in love with him instantly. Later on, he told me that he felt the same way.

So I guess Frieda was implying that there was an attractive new bachelor in our church. Other girls in our congregation had their eyes on Guenther. When he showed an interest in me, I felt a little uneasy, because I did not know how Guenther felt about the other girls. But he soon assured me that he had no interest in them—they were just friends. Then I relaxed and we started dating.

It was January 1948. I was twenty years old, with my twenty-first birthday coming in June. At that time girls my age looked forward to married life. One did not think of putting off getting married in favor of a career. We got engaged on the twenty-fifth of September that same year and got married August 20, 1949.

When I think about the weddings of my children and grandchildren, I have mixed feelings. I am sad because I realize all the things that were missing at our wedding. But I look back with fondness of our courtship in such a turbulent time as it was in Germany after the war.

We had nothing extra—not even a room for the reception. I made my own wedding dress, and Guenther borrowed a suit from a relative. Never mind not having a room for the reception—we did not even have a church yet!

It is a custom in Germany to go before a justice of the peace for a civil ceremony and to get the marriage license. After that the couple could have a church wedding, if they so desired (by law it is not necessary anymore). So, since we did not have a church, our pastor performed the ceremony in our living room.

There were about twenty-five or thirty people—just the immediate family and some relatives. It was a simple affair. My parents did what they could to have a meal and dessert right there.

We really did not need much. We were happy. It also felt good to be surrounded by all the familiar faces after all the separations we experienced during the war. Again, as with Traute and Herbert's wedding, my parents gave up one of their rooms, until we found an apartment.

For our honeymoon, we went to the famous Gruga Gardens. All the flowers were in full bloom, and we enjoyed strolling hand in hand along the garden path. There is really little that matters when you are a newlywed, except being with the one you love!

Frieda

What a relief that life began to be normal again after six years of war. Church life, again, was part of our family—I liked that. In the summertime the churches organized youth conferences at which young people from various other cities would meet and fellowship and worship together.

For one of those conferences, a small group of young people from our congregation in Gelsenkirchen went to Wattenscheid, which was just a few stops away on the streetcar. That was our main mode of transportation.

In between the worship services and concerts, we had breaks where we could mingle and meet the youth groups from other cities. One time I was sitting on a bench next to a handsome young man. I had never seen him before, but later he told me something strange.

He said an inner voice told him, *Helmut, you are sitting next to your future wife*. Then he—kind of—took a closer look to see who I was. He introduced himself and I introduced myself in return. But that was it for our first meeting.

Helmut had just been released from a prisoner of war camp in England. He was ready to get married but thought I looked too young. He was twenty-five years old and I was eighteen—a difference of seven years.

I had a job in Essen at the time. That was also the city in which Helmut's family lived. I started attending the youth group at his church. In one of our youth group meetings, he related to us how life was as a prisoner in a war camp in Florida, USA. He told us that near the prison camp was an orange plantation. The owner of that plantation was allowed to pick up the prisoners and have them work in the plantation and bring them back to the barracks at night.

The plantation owner was also a construction contractor. When he found out that Helmut was a carpenter by trade, he recruited him to work on construction jobs.

As Helmut talked about his experiences from that time, his blue eyes shone, revealing an inner happiness. He was so thankful that as a prisoner of war, he was not mistreated or confined in the camps, but was able to work at what he liked to do. Would you believe despite being captive, he fell in love with the United States of America? (Little did we know this love would change the destiny of the entire family.)

Listening to his story, I could not keep my eyes away from him. I believe I fell in love with him that night.

Sometime later, after another youth group meeting, he asked me, "Can I walk you home today?"

Now it so happened that I was staying with my aunt and uncle because of my job. So I said to Helmut, "Yes, you can take me home, but I am staying here in Essen, because of my job."

We took our time walking to my aunt's house. When we were saying good night, he asked me if we could start dating. I felt like jumping in the air for joy, but restrained myself and just said yes.

After some time, he took me to meet his parents. Many years later, my mother-in-law told me that Helmut's father said to her, "Your daughter-in-law was in our house today."

Helmut's father was a quiet but observant man and a wonderful Christian.

When we started dating, Helmut told me right away that his family had plans to immigrate to America. He asked how I felt about that. Well, I was deeply in love with him and told him that I would go with him wherever he would go.

My sister Elsbeth was dating Guenther at the time, and sometimes we would double date. In September, we both got engaged to our respective boyfriends. Elsbeth and Guenther were married a year later in August 1949.

Helmut and I had our civil ceremony in front of the justice of the peace December 17, 1949. The justice of the peace would issue a marriage license. Once we had that, we were eligible to apply for an apartment. Christians did not live together until after the church wedding. The congregation that Helmut's family attended already had built a new church. So unlike Elsbeth's wedding in our living room, we had a nice ceremony in the new church.

After we settled into our apartment, we started the immigration process. It required a lot of paperwork, a physical examination, and a long interview. This was a time when a substantial number of people wanted to find a better life in the USA. Among them were many refugees from the eastern part of Germany who had lost everything during the war. Many fled the approaching Russian military with just their clothing on their backs and a bundle or a suitcase that was not too cumbersome on the way. Most of these refugees were sponsored to immigrate through churches. Whoever had relatives in the United States used them for their sponsor.

Helmut had an uncle in Benton Harbor, Michigan, who sponsored all the Muellers. This included three of Helmut's brothers, one sister, and Helmut's mother. Unfortunately, Helmut's father passed away before the immigration process was finished. I was the first from the Lenk family to arrive in America, on September 17, 1951.

In the next ten years, most of the rest of the family also came over. But not all.

Church conference after the war

Chapter 20
My Conversion

Helga

Soon after the war ended, free evangelical Christians yearned to start regular worship services again. The first thing on the agenda among the leadership was to find out how many members from various congregations were displaced from their homes and cities.

I recall the pastor coming to our house, because my father was an elder in our church. The two of them were brainstorming where to begin. They started with the people they knew and where they lived. The obvious thing to do was to start with house churches.

Before long, word spread and people contacted each other and worship services started up again. Little congregations sprang up here and there. Papa's musical talent on the table zither came in handy in our meetings. Playing the zither and singing with his wonderful tenor voice, he led the congregational singing.

The next step was to call for a general conference. Essen was chosen for the first big conference. The congregation there already had a fairly good-size building. People came from all over Europe for this great occasion. The conference was held for a whole week.

In 1947, Elsbeth, Frieda, and Fritz took the streetcar to Essen to a youth conference. After one particular meeting, they came home and told my parents that they were "born again." My parents seemed to be pretty excited about it.

After the initial conference, the leadership decided to hold the conferences annually in August. Schools were closed for the summer break. The high school allowed church members to rent the classrooms for lodging. Simple straw mattresses were laid on the floor, and people brought their own sheets and blankets. Women with small children and girls were in one room, men and boys in another. Bathroom facilities were plenty, but there were only cold-water faucets. As far as I know, nobody cared. People took sponge baths all the time, since the general practice was to take a full bath just once a week.

The overall mood of the people was joyful and hopeful. The horrible years of the war were behind us. We had a new government and restorations were going on all over Germany. People were thankful and praising God for protecting them.

The church set up a soup kitchen to accommodate everybody. They served lunch and dinner. For breakfast, people purchased rolls and coffee at a snack bar nearby.

In 1950, my parents allowed me to stay at the school with my cousins. There were several speakers at the conference. One was known to give emotional sermons. (I am not saying that in a derogatory way—it's just a fact.) Every sermon was followed by an appropriate invitation song.

I remember to this day, "Come to the cross with your burden ..."

My cousin, Ingrid was standing next to me. All of a sudden, she stepped forward and responded to the altar call! It only took me a minute or two to follow. I cried as I asked Jesus to come into my heart. I was born again!

How many sins had I committed as an eleven-year-old? That really did not matter. I understood the simple message that if I wanted to go to heaven, I needed Jesus as my Savior. With us was also the daughter of one of the preachers answering the call. The three of us huddled together later and talked about what we had done. We felt pretty good!

Two years later I was baptized by immersion. I can see the church in my mind's eye. There was a lot of wood inside the church. The pulpit, the benches, and the choir loft—all wood. (We had rented this church, because our church did not have a baptistery.) The choir sang, "Holy, holy, holy, holy is the Lord ..." It was a moving and memorable experience.

Chapter 21
Happenings on Both Sides of the Ocean

Helga

Frieda and Helmut adjusted well in their new country. Since Helmut was a carpenter, he had no trouble finding employment. Frieda settled down with their new baby boy as a stay-at-home mom. But she missed her family back in Germany and wrote many letters to us and Elsbeth. In her letters she explained that Guenther, as a chemist, would also find work easily. Eventually, she persuaded Elsbeth and Guenther to immigrate to America. Evidently Frieda's words had the desired effect. They soon started the immigration process.

Manfred was out of school at the time and still did not want to learn a trade, because he lost so much time in his primary school years. Once he graduated from eighth grade, he did not want to hear anything about learning. No trade school, no apprenticeship—he just wanted to work in the coal mines and make money.

This broke my father's heart, and the two of them had many heated arguments. My father warned, "Your health will be ruined in no time. Look at me, my health is ruined already!" Black lung disease is awful. It is accompanied by wretched coughing spasm, and a person affected by it has a tough time breathing.

The labor laws in Germany stated that a person had to be sixteen years of age to work in the underground mine. Up to the time of their sixteenth birthday, young men who chose to be miners worked on a conveyer belt to pick out rocks and other debris mixed in with the coal. Manfred had just turned sixteen in July 1953—the year my sister and her husband wanted to immigrate to the USA. Now Papa thought it would be a good idea for Manfred to go with them. He preferred to send his son away from home rather than have his health ruined like his was. Manfred was not opposed to that idea, and the matter was settled. When the three of them left, we were very sad—most of all me.

From six siblings, there were only two left at home—Fritz and I. Traute still lived in Austria with her husband, Herbert, and their son, Manfred.

A keen observer could tell that Fritz had a calling from God. He studied the Bible and taught Sunday school and seemed to enjoy it. Our pastor encouraged my parents to let Fritz go to a Bible school. They agreed to it, and Fritz was eager to go. Now I was the only one left with my parents. In my heart, I knew I would eventually follow my siblings, but I had to finish my apprenticeship first.

A short time after the three siblings left home, Papa suffered a heart attack. This was before Fritz had left for the Bible school. Fritz took his bike and rode as fast as he could to get our family physician. Ambulances were still not used very much, but doctors did make house calls. The heart attack was not fatal, but left Papa an invalid. After some time, the insurance company thought he could work part time, because he was in his early fifties—too young to retire. They gave him a job in the mine canteen, but he was really too weak, and he had to give that up.

Papa loved to visit the shut-ins and the sick members of our congregation. This was a time after Billy Graham had held one of his first crusades in Europe. Radio stations started broadcasting religious programs. Papa bought himself a tape recorder and taped some new gospel songs. He took the tape recorder to the people he visited and played the songs for them.

The problem was that the first tape recorders were very heavy. Papa managed to take them to the people, but often told me to pick him up and carry the recorder for him.

He was embarrassed when he was walking and had to stop to catch his breath. He actually looked good. He had rosy cheeks and was rather corpulent, but the condition of his heart and lungs really limited his physical activity.

As the black lung disease progressed, the coughing spasms increased also. This was worse at night. Papa decided that it would be better for the rest of the family— mother, Grandma and I—for him to sleep on the first level in the living room. That way he would not disturb us as much when he had to get up.

I have no medical training whatsoever, so I do not know what can be done for black lung disease, but I remember something odd. Our family doctor prescribed cognac for my father. He actually had to go to the local *Apotheke* (pharmacy). I assume it helped loosen the phlegm. Needless to say, Papa was never tempted to misuse it.

Chapter 22
Entering the Job Market

Helga

I finished my eighth grade of school in the spring of 1954. It was time for me to enter the job market. Every time I look back at that year, a little sadness creeps into my heart, because my mother was in America at that time.

Both of my sisters were expecting babies—Elsbeth's second and Frieda's third. Since both of them were expecting in the same month, they thought it would be a good idea if Mother could come over and help with their respective new arrivals. That's how it happened that Mama was away from home when I needed her the most—or so I felt.

I was entering a new phase in my life. Mama was always there for me, even when I needed money for extra classes at school. When there was a lot of coming, and going, Mama was always around. Especially when we were running to bomb shelters and when we were evacuated. But now she was on the other side of the ocean!

My girlfriend Ursula and I decided to go together and look for a job in the retail business.

My other girlfriend Edith—Willy's sister--already worked as a salesgirl in her parent's store. Edith's father had come home from the war and re-opened the butcher shop he had before he was called up for active duty. He was devastated to hear what happened to his boy! Willy could have helped in the business if he were still alive. Now one of Edith's cousins took his place. Edith helped out in the store even while she was still in school.

Being salesgirls appealed to Ursula and me. So off we went from store to store to see if we could find an apprenticeship. It did not take long until we both found employment. Ursula was hired in a light and electric supply store. I found a job in a grocery store. To be a salesgirl required an apprenticeship. Even in a grocery store, we needed to know more than just ringing up items on a cash register.

We worked five days and attended vocational school one day a week. (We still had the forty-eight-hour week.) We learned about the products we were selling, where they came from, a little about import and export, bookkeeping, and advertising. It was a comprehensive education in the retail business.

An apprentice was bound by a contract and got paid on an escalating scale. The first year was the lowest, the second a little higher, with the third year the highest salary.

Starting out, one would work under a *Geselle* (a journeyman or skilled worker— the next step up from apprentice) or work under a master. The experienced workers liked to tease the new hireling. For instance, someone told me, "Helga, please bring the wooden scissors to the boss." (Wooden scissors?)

Another thing is that I had to perform other duties than selling groceries. During the day when traffic in the store was minimal, my boss-lady sent me to do some cleaning in her home. Was it legal? I did not question it—I just obeyed.

Later my employers (a husband and wife) wanted to start a new store in Gelsenkirchen-Horst—the small town I lived in. Normally I took the streetcar to and from the main store, but when my boss wanted to work in the new store to get things ready, he took me on his motorcycle, and I would help him with whatever was needed to be done for the store's grand opening. This consisted of cleaning up after the construction crew and assisting my boss in building storage shelves. I guess an apprentice was being taken advantage of, but I did not mind because I could walk home after the work was done. After the store opened, I worked there and did not have to travel to the main store anymore. That was convenient.

The store hours were long. We worked from 8:30 a.m. until 1 p.m., at which time the store closed for lunch break. Then it reopened from 3 p.m. until 6:30 p.m. That is how I started. In the second or third year of my apprenticeship, the forty-eight-hour week was reduced to forty-five hours. That meant only five hours on Saturdays.

I liked working as a salesgirl. Grocery shopping was so different from what it is today. First of all, having a refrigerator was unheard of. Some people had iceboxes with block ice, but most people did not even have that. People shopped more often for fresh items such as dairy, meat, or produce. Our store did have one refrigerator unit where we kept lunchmeats and other items that needed to be kept cold. Not every grocery store sold milk—ours did not. For our home, Mother went to a different store. She usually bought only what she needed within a short time. The milk needed to be boiled right away, since it was not homogenized.

The busiest shopping day was when it was payday at the local coal mine. Then customers came with their prepared lists. On those days the store was crowded, and people had to wait in long lines. When it was the customer's turn, she read the items and quantity to the salesclerk, who in turn wrote everything on a sales slip. After that, the clerk gathered all the items and entered the price next to the products. Not everything was prepackaged. Sugar and flour, for instance, had to be weighed to what the order called for.

On payday the lists could be long, and the salesgirl had to add all the prices in her head—calculators were not available yet.

Credit cards were not used either at the time. However, not everybody managed their money so it would last from paycheck to paycheck. What was the answer in those cases?

The accepted custom was that local stores extended credit to their customers. We, as the clerks, had to watch that the amount was not getting out of hand.

Unfortunately, there were times when people owed us money and did not return to our store, but shopped elsewhere. This is a part I did not like about working for a private owner. My boss would send me to people's homes to try to collect the debts. In today's world, that really sounds strange! Picture this: A teenage girl knocks on someone's door and tries to collect money—that would just not happen today.

In our two-hour lunchtime, we often stayed in the storage area in the back of the store. We had a little electric hot plate on which we cooked simple meals—sometimes two courses in progression. We exchanged the latest novels and spent the time enjoying ourselves.

When I was in my third year of my apprenticeship, my boss sold the store. The new owner wanted all the employees to stay. Our new boss brought in more fresh produce. He also went to the open-air farmer's market twice a week. We had nothing to do with that. However, the hours of the open market were usually from 9 a.m. until 1 p.m.

That meant that he came back when it was our lunch break. He expected us to help him unload the truck. Sometimes we did it, sometimes we went out for lunch to avoid working during our break (he could not really force us to do so). One time he found us in the local ice cream parlor. He looked at us and then picked up the bill for our ice cream. He was really a nice employer.

Soon my third year was up and I was ready to take the *Gesellen Prüfung* (the exam for the next vocational level). We had to take a written exam as well as an oral examination in front of a panel from the Industry and Merchant Association. I had no problems and brought home a good grade.

My boss was proud of me, because he was a young man just starting out in the retail business. I was the first employee to graduate. He rewarded me by taking me to downtown Essen. A new kind of grocery store was making its entrance in Germany that he wanted me to see.

It was 1957 when I finished my apprenticeship, and the retail business had undergone tremendous changes. By now we had frozen food available. It started with frozen vegetables and progressed from there to a variety of merchandise. The store in Essen had several freezers and little shopping carts. I enjoyed the trip very much, and my boss bought me a little flower vase to remember the occasion. I still have it after all these years.

New Merchandise

Among other new merchandise coming into our store was wine and beer. The evidence of the *Wirtschaftswunder* (economic miracle) made itself known. People now could afford to have a glass of wine or beer with their meal, if they had a taste for it. The salesgirls were supposed to be knowledgeable about the store's merchandise. Sometimes I wonder even today what I told the customers! I was only seventeen years old. What did I know about wine?

New merchandise also aroused our curiosity. So, when a new shipment included champagne, we decided to try it. Our employer had two stores and spent most of his time at the main store. At the second store, we were four employees. Two advanced salesgirls and two apprentices. We managed the store in his absence. So here we were with the newest item for sale. We knew that opening a champagne bottle was a little tricky, but that did not keep us from trying. Just when we had the cork a little lose, we heard the boss coming into the store. One of us took the bottle and ran into the basement, put it into a bucket and put something heavy on it.

It was 6:30 p.m., and we were ready to close the store. Our employer wanted to pick up the money and see how everything was going. We assured him that everything was fine, but inside we were all rattled up! What if the cork came out by itself and sprayed champagne all over the basement? Somehow, we managed to appear calm and normal. We gave him the money, closed the storefront door and went on our way—he in his truck and the four of us walking, as if going to the streetcar stop.

As soon as his truck disappeared into the distance, we went back to the store. Because the oldest salesgirl was in charge of opening and closing the store, she had a key. We went into the store and closed the rolling shutter door behind us. Then we proceeded into the storage area to check on our bottle.

I don't even recall what happened afterwards. I have a feeling we just pushed the cork back in. We were not in the mood to celebrate, but I do remember feeling guilty of almost being caught in a crime! (Well, let's just say it was something we were not supposed to do.)

I had another schoolmate who also finished her apprenticeship and now worked in another store. She told me that she received more money than I was making and urged me to switch jobs. In Germany, the salary for a *Geselle* was fixed by the unions and the industry, but employers could pay more if they so desired. I took my girlfriend's advice and changed my job. I worked there for two years until I immigrated to the United States.

Teen Years in Germany

What were the years like as a teenager in the mid-fifties? Of course, life was not all work. The most natural thing anywhere in this world for teenagers is girls discover boys and boys discover girls.

However, the fifties were different from anything after the sexual revolution in the late sixties and early seventies. (Think *The Waltons*.) As far as I know, none of my friends were sexually active. We often went out in groups. Watching a soccer match was a big thing. Since we did not have a television set, we went to the milk bar or an ice cream parlor to watch a game. Those were our hangout places. Of course, we also tried alcohol, but even that was never out of control. The drinking age in Germany was sixteen, but none of us could afford very much.

The biggest attractions were the movie theaters. German studios produced good pictures, but I was drawn to movies that were filmed on American soil. In my youthful fantasies, I convinced myself that by watching those films, I could get a glimpse of what America looked like. Among the imported Hollywood movies, I recollect seeing crime dramas staged in the big cities in the United States, and western movies that showed the countryside. I was looking forward to immigrating.

Movies were expensive. Even though I worked, I had to give part of my money to my parents. That was just the way things were done. When children brought in some money, they had to help with the household expenses. Saturday night was the preferred time to see a movie. I was usually done with my job before Edith. When I went to meet her and the family was still cleaning up the store, I helped them. Her parents were generous people. They gave Edith a little more money so she could pay for my movie, too. For that, I didn't mind cleaning at all.

Edith had a boyfriend, but they didn't mind if I went along to the movie occasionally. Other times I went with Ursula. When one of us was dating someone, we just went our separate ways. All three of us girls broke up the relationship if the boys got too aggressive. Everybody knew girls who "did it," but the three of us were not among them. I was not surprised when I went to a class reunion in 1979 and heard that one classmate was already a grandmother! We were all turning forty that year.

A girl named Linda lived across from the street from us. Linda was a year older than I. We spent a lot of time in our younger years together, just because we were close neighbors and participated in group games. Now Linda took dancing lessons. Occasionally, the students could bring a guest. Yes, you guessed it, I went along. I enjoyed the dances, but did not know how to dance. Linda showed me a few basic steps at home. Then at the dance, I asked someone, "What is the band playing? And what are the steps?"

The dances, of course, were ballroom dances—waltz, tango, foxtrot, etc. I liked the musical rhythm. As long as I kept my curfew, my parents did not ask me every night where I spent my time. I say that because in my parents' opinion, dancing was not something a Christian girl participated in.

On Sundays, I regularly attended our worship services, and I liked our small youth group. After our Bible Study, which was led by my cousin, we spent the time playing games. My cousin also taught us many songs. Sometimes we sang them at the youth conferences.

Those conferences were a lot of fun. Young people gathered from other cities to wherever the host church was located. Every youth group had their own choir. It was spiritually uplifting to sing in a choir and also to listen to others perform beautiful songs accompanied by piano or guitars. Another popular instrument in Germany was the accordion. I believe Germans are known for their love of music.

Besides the singing and listening to sermons, we also did sightseeing in the surrounding areas. That gave us the opportunity to mingle with young people from other cities and get to know each other. Many have found their life partners at those conferences. That was the case with Frieda and Helmut.

But I was too young to be thinking about marriage.

Chapter 23
My Last Three Years in Germany

Helga

A lot of changes took place in the last three years of my life in Germany. My sister Traute, who moved to Austria after marrying Herbert, also decided to immigrate to the United States. By then their son was eleven. The three of them joined my other siblings in the early spring of 1956.

My brother Fritz graduated from Bible school and came back home. He was twenty-six years old and ready to enter the ministry. Fritz received a letter from a pastor in Philadelphia, USA, stating that a pastoral position was open in Union City, New Jersey. Would he be interested in it?

Another question was, would Renate, whom he was dating, be willing to come with him? Yes, she was. They decided to get married first. Fritz and Renate joined their hearts in matrimony on December 22, 1956 — that makes it 60 years as of this writing!

Together they immigrated also in 1957.

Now I was the only one of the Lenk siblings left in Germany. It would be only a matter of time until I would make the journey.

Mama and Papa were not ready to leave Germany yet, because my Grandmother was still living with us. Papa felt obligated to stay until her time on this earth ended.

In the meantime, I had changed my job for a better position in another store. This store was located closer to Gelsenkirchen. When a town did not have a certain number of inhabitants, it was connected to a bigger city. Hence our town was Gelsenkirchen-Horst.

My new place of employment was between the two cities.

When I heard that English language courses were offered at a night school in Gelsenkirchen, I signed up. I was sure that would come in handy to get a job in the United States. This earned me the nickname "Miss America" from my co-workers.

Grandma told my parents to go ahead and follow the children. She often expressed her thoughts by saying, "Death is standing at my door. I am going to see my Savior very soon face to face." Three of my grandmother's married daughters lived in close proximity. Aunt Liese was living only three houses away from us and said she would be glad to take her mother in. Her children were all married and out of the house, so she had the room.

Papa said I should start my papers, and that he and Mama would follow soon. Most of the time it was a drawn-out process to get the background and health checks, but my papers came relatively fast. For one thing, at nineteen I was too young to have been in the Nazi party (a major hindrance in coming to America), and I was healthy, meaning I could work and provide for myself. Every immigrant still needed a sponsor, and my brother-in-law, Guenther, gladly took on that role. I had my ticket in my hand in eight months.

As the time of my departure came closer, my excitement grew more and more. In one of her letters, Frieda stated that one could buy ice cream in a supermarket in half-gallon sizes. What a treat!

It was a little sad saying goodbye to all my friends, but I was also filled with anticipation of what the future would hold for me.

Finally, the day arrived—I would be going to America! My flight was from Cologne via Switzerland to New York. My parents accompanied me to the airport. In the waiting area, we had a touching moment. This was goodbye between parents and child.

As a teenager, I was not always obedient. On the other hand, I felt that my parents had also made mistakes. Isn't that typical thinking of a teenager? Whatever the case may be, my father took the initiative. "Do we have to say anything to each other?"

I have forgotten the words that were spoken, but it is sufficient to know that we hugged each other and let the peace and presence of God enfold us.

Epilogue

Helga

My parents started their immigration process soon after I left. Grandma moved in with my aunt. However, in 1960 we received the sad news that my father had passed away. By that time, they had all the papers ready and even had the tickets.

Since all my siblings had growing families, none of them had extra money to go to the funeral. I was still single and therefore it would be the easiest for me to take off from work. We all pooled our money for my ticket.

Fritz was still serving as a minister in the church in New Jersey. He also decided to fly to Germany and be at my mother's side.

I was shocked at my father's appearance. He had lost a lot of weight and his skin looked—well—lifeless. My one consolation was that I knew his heart, and my heart assured me that he went to heaven.

In his almost forty years in the service of God, Fritz had moved to Michigan, Wisconsin and Nebraska. While he lived in Nebraska, he worked at the German Unity Press. This small publishing company produced a monthly newsletter called *Die Evangeliums Posaune* (The Gospel Trumpet). In every issue, Fritz wrote a little sermonette. He concentrated on the First Letter of Peter. Eventually it was published as a commentary in 1970. It was well received in German-speaking congregations in the United States.

I had the privilege of translating it from German into English. It was published with the title: *Feed My Sheep* in 2014 by Westbow Press, a division of Thomas Nelson and Zondervan. Fritz is now retired and lives with his wife Renate in Edmonton, Alberta, Canada.

At the funeral, I helped my mother pack up whatever she wanted to take to America. I stayed a little longer than Fritz. As a matter of fact, we arranged for me to come back on my father's ticket. My parents had scheduled their journey on an ocean liner. This gave me the opportunity to also experience a sea voyage.

I was sharing an apartment with another German girl, and we decided to get a bigger apartment and take my mother in. My roommate eventually moved out, but my mother and I lived together until I got married in 1962. From that time on Mama lived with my sister Elsbeth until the Lord took her home in 1989—she was eighty-eight years old.

Traute, Elsbeth, Frieda, and Manfred, with their respective spouses, settled in Michigan. Guenther was a choir director for many years. Elsbeth taught Sunday school and Frieda played the organ in the church. Helmut was on the board of elders and used his carpentry craft on several mission trips.

Eslbeth, Frieda, Helmut, and I sang in Guenther's choir. That is when we remembered the most about Papa's love for music. How he played the zither and led the family in singing. He truly set a good example of what it means to have the joy of the Lord in your heart.

My mother and I relocated to New Jersey. There I met my husband, Arnold. We were married for fifty-two years until he left this earth in 2014. Mother had already moved back to Michigan to live with Elsbeth. I moved to Virginia to be closer to our two daughters.

Of six siblings, only four are still alive. Traute died in 1997, preceded by her husband. Manfred had a fatal automobile accident when he was only forty-two years old. He left behind his wife, Christa, and two children.

Elsbeth, Frieda, and I are widows. Fritz and Renate celebrated their sixtieth wedding anniversary on December 22, 2016.

Many years have passed since all of us came to the United States. I have nieces and nephews who are grandparents already. I hope they will enjoy reading the background of the Lenk family.

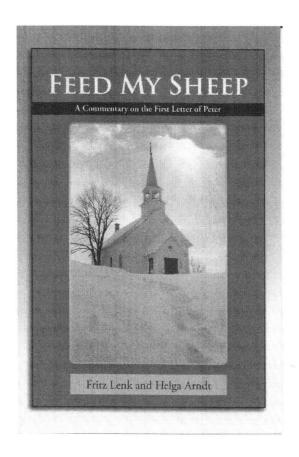

The letter of 1 Peter is sometimes also known as "the letter of the living hope." It is a letter written by a godly shepherd who wants to make sure his flock has good instructions on how to live a godly life. The author is Peter, one of Jesus' twelve disciples. Silas was Peter's scribe.

Right at the start, the apostle describes the wonderful inheritance "that can never perish, spoil or face." Then he give practical advice on how to attain maturity in Christ. Topics range from holy living, obedience to authorities, family relations, and instructions for church elders. It further touches on such subjects as suffering injustice at the hand of men and suffering for Jesus' sake.

Rev. Lenk explains all of the above in a phrase by phrase commentary. It is an excellent tool for spiritual growth. It can also be used as a devotional.

Available from WestBow Press
www.westbowpress.com
This title may also be ordered through your local bookseller
or preferred on-line retailer.

Made in the USA
Middletown, DE
03 June 2017